CONSTRUCTION

ELECTRIFICATION

C.C.C. CAMPS

SHELTER BELT

FLOOD CONTROL

RELIEF

THE **LIFE** HISTORY OF THE UNITED STATES

Volume 11: 1933-1945

NEW DEAL AND GLOBAL WAR

THE LIFE HISTORY OF THE UNITED STATES

THE **LIFE** HISTORY OF THE UNITED STATES

Consulting Editor, Henry F. Graff

Volume 11: 1933-1945

NEW DEAL AND GLOBAL WAR

by William E. Leuchtenburg

and the Editors of LIFE

TIME INCORPORATED, NEW YORK

THE AUTHOR of Volume 11 of this series, William E. Leuchtenburg, has concentrated on the study of the United States during the 20th Century. At present Professor of American History at Columbia University, he has taught at Smith College, New York University and Harvard. During the summer of 1956, Dr. Leuchtenburg lectured at the Salzburg Seminar for American Studies in Austria, and in 1961-1962 he was a Fellow at the Center for Advanced Study in the Behavioral Sciences, Stanford, California. He is the author of *The Perils of Prosperity, 1914-1932,* and won the 1964 Bancroft Prize for *Franklin D. Roosevelt and the New Deal, 1932-1940.*

THE CONSULTING EDITOR for this series, Henry F. Graff, is Chairman of the Department of History at Columbia University.

TIME-LIFE BOOKS

EDITOR *Norman P. Ross*
TEXT DIRECTOR *William Jay Gold*   ART DIRECTOR *Edward A. Hamilton*
CHIEF OF RESEARCH *Beatrice T. Dobie*

Editorial staff for Volume 11
THE LIFE HISTORY OF THE UNITED STATES

SERIES EDITOR *Sam Welles*
ASSISTANT EDITOR *Jerry Korn*
DESIGNERS *Douglas R. Steinbauer, Frank Crump*
STAFF WRITERS *John Stanton, Gerald Simons, Alfred Lansing,*
Peter Meyerson, Sam Halper
CHIEF RESEARCHER *Clara E. Nicolai*
RESEARCHERS *Terry Drucker, Mary Youatt, Ruth Silva, Ellen Leiman,*
Elizabeth Collins, Evelyn Hauptman, Jacqueline Coates, Joan Scafarello
PICTURE RESEARCHERS *Margaret K. Goldsmith, Theo Pascal*
ART ASSOCIATE *Robert L. Young*
ART ASSISTANTS *James D. Smith, Wayne R. Young, Douglas B. Graham*
COPY STAFF *Marian Gordon Goldman, Gail Weesner, Dolores A. Littles*

PUBLISHER *Rhett Austell*
GENERAL MANAGER *John A. Watters*

LIFE MAGAZINE

EDITOR   MANAGING EDITOR   PUBLISHER
Edward K. Thompson   *George P. Hunt*   *Jerome S. Hardy*

Valuable assistance in the preparation of this volume was given by Roger Butterfield, picture consultant; Doris O'Neil, Chief of the LIFE Picture Library; Richard M. Clurman, Chief of the TIME-LIFE News Services; and Content Peckham, Chief of the Time Inc. Bureau of Editorial Reference.

THE COVER depicts Churchill and Roosevelt, both looking fairly chipper the morning after a huge Russian banquet with some 45 toasts. This is a detail from the official Yalta Conference photograph that appears on page 140.

CONTENTS

1. THE FIRST HUNDRED DAYS

SINCE 1789 the United States has undergone two major revolutions. One was the Civil War, the other was the Great Depression of the 1930s. Each crisis marked the culmination of decades of tumultuous change; each jeopardized the nation's future; each bequeathed a legacy to the American people. The Depression, coming as the anticlimax of 70 years of industrialization, threatened to sever the bonds that held together an infinitely complex civilization. It led, finally, to the creation of the welfare state—and to the enduring problems of big government and new conflicts of classes and interests.

The shock of the Depression was especially great because men had come to believe in the previous decade that the country had achieved "a permanent plateau of prosperity." In August 1928 Herbert Hoover had declared, apparently with good reason: "We in America today are nearer to the final triumph over poverty than ever before in the history of any land."

Fourteen months later the crash of the stock market shattered this prosperity, with reverberations that were felt throughout the Western world. By the end of 1932, American industry was operating at less than half its 1929 volume. For every four automobiles that had rolled off the assembly line in 1929, only one was turned out in 1932. Construction of office buildings halted so abruptly that some were left with naked girders rusting in the open air. Foreign trade slumped: Merchant ships carried outbound cargoes worth $5.2 billion in 1929 but only $1.6 billion in 1932. Blue-chip stocks fell, U.S. Steel

CAREWORN AND ILL after 12 years as President, Franklin D. Roosevelt still shows the confidence that inspired America when he first tackled the problems of the Depression.

from 262 to 22, American Can from 182 to 30. As crop prices plunged, many a farmer saw the labor of a lifetime wiped out and his fields, his house and his equipment put under the sheriff's hammer.

There were more than 13 million unemployed—a staggering 25 per cent of the labor force. Of these, no one knew how many were wandering the country by the summer of 1932; certainly one million, perhaps two, including an estimated 200,000 young boys and girls. In 1932 the Southern Pacific ejected 683,000 trespassers seeking shelter in its cars, most of them young men from 16 to 25. By the end of the year the railroad had surrendered to the "Vagabond Army" and was adding empty freight cars to accommodate them.

Jobless and homeless, thousands of the unemployed built makeshift shelters in empty lots in the big cities. Men spent their days scavenging for food, the winter nights trying to find warmth. Literary critic Edmund Wilson reported: "There is not a garbage-dump in Chicago which is not diligently haunted by the hungry. Last summer in the hot weather when the smell was sickening and the flies were thick, there were a hundred people a day coming to one of the dumps, falling on the heap of refuse as soon as the truck had pulled out and digging in it with sticks and hands."

Most Americans escaped such extreme privation, but there were few who did not know the fear that their turn might come next. Among the unemployed on Detroit's relief rolls, Mayor Frank Murphy reported, were doctors, lawyers, 45 ministers and "two families after whom streets are named." "The year 1931," the historian Arnold Toynbee said, "was distinguished from previous years . . . by one outstanding feature. In 1931, men and women all over the world were seriously contemplating and frankly discussing the possibility that the Western system of Society might break down and cease to work."

THE crash broke up America's 50-year romance with the businessman. Many corporation leaders realized they did not know how to fight the Depression, and after a time the country sensed this. Marriner Eccles, who headed a Utah economic empire, wrote that his friends, his family and the community all expected him "to find the way out of the pit," but he felt helpless: "Night after night . . . I would return home exhausted by the pretensions of knowledge I was forced to wear in a daytime masquerade."

The social attitudes of some business leaders aroused great popular indignation. Men like Charles Mitchell, whose National City Bank had provided its speculating officers with interest-free loans that ultimately came out of the pockets of its stockholders, and Samuel Insull, whose utility empire collapsed, ruining thousands of small investors, were singled out for special censure. Moreover, many Americans for the first time came to question the claims of the capitalist system itself and to take a second look at Soviet Russia. The left-wing New Republic said: "Her pains are growing pains, ours seem to be those of dissolution." In the 1932 election, an impressive array of American writers—Sherwood Anderson, John Dos Passos, Theodore Dreiser, Erskine Caldwell—publicly supported the Communist ticket.

The assault on businessmen and on capitalism implied a specific rebuke to President Hoover and to his way of thinking. Hoover had approached the Depression with ideas springing from the individualistic tradition nourished in pioneer America. He had insisted that the federal government should not provide relief to the unemployed, and he had argued that private charity and

Louis McHenry Howe, personal secretary who was said to be "the man behind Roosevelt," works at his White House desk. Howe encouraged Roosevelt to return to politics after his polio attack. Labeled a "kingmaker," Howe quipped: "It's no trick to make a President. Give me a man who stays reasonably sober, shaves and wears a clean shirt every day."

local government would meet the needs of the impoverished. In 1932 these convictions were subject to a popular mandate. "This election," the President observed, "is not a mere shift from the ins to the outs. It means deciding the direction our nation will take over a century to come."

Hoover's opponent, Franklin Delano Roosevelt, did not join issue with the President directly. Indeed, much of Roosevelt's campaign was disturbingly vague, and his speeches on fiscal policy were a welter of contradictions. In words that were to seem almost comical in retrospect, he stated: "I accuse the present Administration of being the greatest spending Administration in peace times in all our history." And yet, by his actions as governor of New York, Roosevelt had indicated a willingness to use the power of government that distinguished his ideas from Hoover's. He had created the first comprehensive system of unemployment relief in the nation, had expanded development of public power and had sponsored a broad program for social welfare. "The country needs and, unless I mistake its temper, the country demands bold, persistent experimentation," the governor asserted.

Roosevelt was elected overwhelmingly. Now he had to back his vigorous words with action. He faced a fearful number of tasks. He had to restore the shattered economy. He had to give a new sense of purpose to the federal government and enlist it on behalf of a national interest more basic than that of business or any other single group. But most of all he had to restore the faith of a nation that seemed almost palsied by fear. Charles M. Schwab of Bethlehem Steel was quoted as saying: "I'm afraid; every man is afraid."

The baseball writer Rud Rennie recalled his journey north with the New York Yankees from their training camp in 1933: "We came home that year through Southern cities which looked as though they had been ravaged by an invisible enemy. People seemed to be in hiding. They even would not come out to see Babe Ruth and Lou Gehrig. . . . Birmingham, a once-thriving, bright metropolis, looked as if it had been swept by a plague."

Sporadic outbursts of violence led some to wonder if the country was faced with the menace of revolution. In Iowa farmers, bent on halting the marketing of crops in order to boost prices, nearly sealed off the area around Sioux City. Protests against mortgage foreclosures grew so angry that sheriffs had to halt auctions. In Wisconsin dairy farmers dumped milk on the highways in an effort to reduce the supplies going to market.

THE muted violence of the winter found one dramatic expression. On February 15 the President-elect was chatting in crowded Bay Front Park in Miami with Mayor Anton Cermak of Chicago when Giuseppe Zangara, a deranged bricklayer, fired five shots at them with a pistol. As he started to shoot, the wife of a Miami doctor shoved his arm up. The assassin missed Roosevelt, but wounded Cermak and four others. Roosevelt displayed great courage throughout the incident. He refused to leave and took Cermak into his own car. "I held him all the way to the hospital," Roosevelt reported afterward. "It seemed like 25 miles. . . . I remember I said, 'Tony, don't move—keep quiet —it won't hurt if you keep quiet and remain perfectly still.' " A few days later Cermak died. Zangara was executed a month after the shooting.

Since Election Day, Roosevelt had been working on drafts of legislation with members of his "brain trust," including political scientist Raymond Moley, agricultural expert Rexford Guy Tugwell and Adolf Berle Jr., an expert

Utilities magnate Samuel Insull is escorted through the gates of Chicago's Cook County Jail during his 1934 mail fraud trial. It ended in acquittal, but Insull was ruined. Though his income in the 1920s exceeded $500,000 a year, at his death in 1938 he left an estate of only $7,600; his creditors realized a mere fraction of a cent on each dollar owed them.

on corporate finance, all of them from the faculty of Columbia University.

Yet many questioned whether Roosevelt had a program that offered much hope of recovery. "No one knows his heart and few have seen behind the masking smile that wreathes his face," observed editor William Allen White of Emporia, Kansas. "We are putting our hands in a grab-bag. Heaven only knows what we shall pull out." A remarkable number of people thought Roosevelt would make a weak President. Writer H. L. Mencken believed him "far too feeble and wishy-washy a fellow to make a really effective fight."

As the time came for him to take office, the long financial illness that had gripped the country took a sudden turn for the worse. In three years, more than 5,000 banks which had overextended their credit resources had shut their doors; nine million savings accounts had vanished. Now banks closed up in every part of the country. On the morning of March 4, inauguration day, brokers in New York's Stock Exchange saw Richard Whitney, their president, mount the rostrum to announce a historic edict: The exchange had closed down. By that day every state in the union had either closed its banks or was letting them operate only on a restricted basis. As the banking system collapsed, all eyes looked toward Washington. It seemed to many that it mattered less how the incoming President acted than that he act. "A fool who can lead is better than a wise man who can fumble," wrote White.

At 1:08 on March 4, 1933, Chief Justice Charles Evans Hughes administered the oath of office to Franklin Roosevelt. Then, as anxious millions gathered around their radio sets, the new President, his chin uplifted, his voice firm, made his first public pronouncement: "First of all, let me assert my firm belief that the only thing we have to fear is fear itself—nameless, unreasoning, unjustified terror. . . . We are stricken by no plague of locusts. Plenty is at our doorstep, but a generous use of it languishes in the very sight of the supply."

He would present Congress with a program of action, but if Congress did not act and the emergency persisted, the President announced, "I shall not evade the clear course of duty that will then confront me. I shall ask the Congress for the one remaining instrument to meet the crisis—broad Executive power to wage a war against the emergency, as great as the power that would be given to me if we were in fact invaded by a foreign foe."

R OOSEVELT'S speech had an electrifying effect. In the next week nearly half a million people wrote to their new President. Americans sensed immediately that they had a leader, one who would act, who would mobilize the power of the government to help them. And indeed Roosevelt moved quickly. His first task was to rehabilitate the nation's banks. On the day after his inauguration, he issued two edicts: One summoned Congress into special session; the other halted transactions in gold and proclaimed a national bank holiday.

The very totality of the holiday helped snap tensions, and the country, with some sense of relief, turned its energies to adjusting to a world without money. Operations that depended on ready cash had a hard time of it. At New York's Radio City *King Kong* played to empty houses. In New Orleans, where hundreds of Mardi Gras visitors were stranded without money, the race track closed down. Madison Square Garden accepted everything from jigsaw puzzles to spark plugs as the price of admission to the Golden Gloves semifinals.

On March 9 the special session of Congress convened in an atmosphere of wartime crisis. A little before one o'clock, Roosevelt's banking message was

The cover of a bootlegger's price list brazenly offers a phone number for would-be purchasers of illegal beverages. Such lists often offered "top brands"—usually diluted, sometimes by up to 80 per cent. Sample prices: Scotch, $2.50 a quart; bourbon, $4.50 for three pints; gin, $3.50 for three quarts.

read to the House. A bill accompanying the message proposed a wide range of presidential powers over banking and arranged for the reopening of those banks with liquid assets and the reorganization of the rest. The members of the House had no printed copies of the bill and had to rely on an explanation presented by Chairman Henry Steagall of the Banking and Currency Committee. The chamber took only 38 minutes to pass the bill—without a word changed. A half hour later the Senate took up the measure. By 7:30 it too had adopted the bill, with only seven dissenting votes. At 8:36, barely seven hours after the bill had been introduced, President Roosevelt signed it into law.

Three days later, in the first of what would become a memorable series of radio "fireside chats," the President assured the people that it was now safe to entrust their savings to the banks. When the banks opened their doors the next morning in the 12 Federal Reserve Bank cities, deposits far exceeded withdrawals. The immediate crisis was over, and the history-making First Hundred Days of the Roosevelt New Deal had begun.

FROM March 9 until Congress adjourned on June 16, President Roosevelt sent 15 separate proposals to Capitol Hill, and Congress adopted all 15. In all, the bills of the Hundred Days represented the most extraordinary set of reforms in the country's history.

The act of March 9 met the immediate banking emergency. By June Congress would enact more far-reaching banking legislation. The Glass-Steagall Act not only separated investment from commercial banking but provided a controversial innovation: federal insurance of deposits. Enacted with grave reservations (on the part of Roosevelt, among others), the guarantee of deposits proved a brilliant success. Among insured banks, suspensions for the rest of the decade totaled less than 8 per cent of the number in 1933 alone.

Among the institutions swept away in the Roosevelt revolution was prohibition. In February 1933, before the new President took office, both houses voted to repeal the 18th Amendment; the measure was sent to the states for ratification. Nine days after he became President, Roosevelt asked Congress to legalize beer by changing the Volstead Act, which defined the "intoxicating liquors" forbidden by the prohibition amendment as any drink with an alcoholic content over .5 per cent. The lawmakers quickly complied. On April 7 beer was sold legally in America for the first time in 13 years; it contained 3.2 per cent alcohol. Before the year was out the 21st Amendment was ratified, and the prohibition era—the era of bootleggers and rumrunners and bathtub gin—was at an end.

Within two weeks after Roosevelt took office, the spirit of the country seemed changed beyond recognition. In that fortnight, wrote columnist Walter Lippmann, the new President had achieved a recapture of morale comparable to that following the second battle of the Marne.

Actually Roosevelt's legislative program had been modest thus far. He had put the nation's finances in order and given the country beer, but he had yet to deal with the besetting problem of recovery. On March 16 the President charted a new course: He asked Congress to take unprecedented action to meet the farm crisis.

He had earlier requested his new Secretary of Agriculture, the Iowa farm editor Henry Agard Wallace, to work out a program of subsidies to farmers who limited their production. In short order Wallace and his aides had drafted

A three-cent stamp issued in 1933 pictures the three-towered Federal Building at Chicago's Century of Progress world's fair, which was a financial success despite the hard times. The fame of the exposition stemmed not so much from the exhibits as from the bare-skin antics of blonde fan dancer Sally Rand.

the Agricultural Adjustment Act, which proposed to restrict acreage, levy a tax on the processors of agricultural commodities (for example, on millers) and pay those growers who agreed to curb production a subsidy based on "parity," a formula which would give the farmer the same level of purchasing power he had had just before World War I.

In essence the new bill would transfer income from the consumer to the farmer; like a protective tariff, it subsidized one part of the population at the expense of the remainder. The New Dealers justified the subsidy by citing the disproportion between farm and industrial prices. An increase in rural income, they said, would mean a great increase in the market for industrial products—it would bring the economy back into balance. Not everyone agreed. Economist Clair Wilcox protested: "The farmers would have more money to spend. The rest of us would have less. Total demand would stay where it is."

Even more disturbing to some were the long-range consequences of such legislation. Although the AAA was intended as a temporary measure, critics warned that its adoption would mark a major departure. "Applied at the outset to four crops, it was extended by the House to seven," Wilcox pointed out. "It will shortly become a permanent part of our governmental machinery." Said Walter Lippmann: "The allotment plan has all the faults of protection and all the complexities of State socialism." But he could see no better remedy.

In May Congress passed the farm bill. By the end of 1935 the government had paid out $1.5 billion in AAA money, and the farmers' net income had risen $3.4 billion. By the war years the farm bloc, once so impotent, would be strong enough to exact up to 113 per cent of parity from the government.

Secretary of the Interior Harold L. Ickes, caricatured by Miguel Covarrubias, was noted for his temper. Ickes detested his middle name, LeClare, but even more he hated having it misspelled—which it often was, as "Le Claire." Roosevelt had his own private name for the irascible Ickes: Donald Duck.

WHILE Congress was debating the farm measures, sentiment for inflation was mounting. In the Senate a bill calling for free coinage of silver (which would have permitted a great increase in the amount of money in circulation) came within 10 votes of passing, and Roosevelt was informed that the next time a similar measure came up it would certainly be enacted. The President, who was beginning by then to entertain certain inflationary ideas of his own, thereupon announced that he would accept an inflationary proposal if it were revised to give him discretionary rather than mandatory powers. Having committed himself to inflation, he almost immediately decided on an even more drastic move. He called 125 newspapermen to the White House to hear a stunning announcement: The United States, for the first time since 1879, was off the gold standard. His aim was to halt falling prices, but he had embraced a policy that deeply alarmed many conservatives. "Maybe the country doesn't know it yet," financier Bernard Baruch said, "but I think we may find that we've been in a revolution more drastic than the French Revolution."

In the fall of 1933 Roosevelt took another inflationary step. After a spurt upward beginning in the spring of 1933, crop prices had cracked again in late summer, and irate farmers talked of marching on Washington. Desperately casting about for some plan of action, Roosevelt embraced a proposal for the purchase of gold at rising prices. The authors of this plan convinced him it would both provide the country a greater share of the world's trade and cause domestic commodity prices to soar as the gold value of the dollar fell. Dean Acheson, Under Secretary of the Treasury, and other orthodox advisers argued against this, but Roosevelt brushed their objections aside. "Gentlemen," he later told his monetary officials, "if we continued a week or so longer without my

As Secretary of Agriculture, Henry A. Wallace occupied a post once held by his father, Henry C., and once declined by his grandfather Henry. The young Henry A. once said, surprisingly, that his ambition was "to make the world safe for corn breeders." He went on to pioneer in developing high-yield corn.

having made this move on gold, we would have had an agrarian revolution in this country." One official quoted him as saying that "for the first time in his memory . . . Wall Street was not dictating the fiscal policy of the government."

But the gold-buying theory did not work out. Wholesale commodity prices actually fell slightly during November and December, farm prices most of all. At the beginning of 1934 Roosevelt decided to halt gold buying and stabilize the dollar. The Gold Reserve Act of that January set an upper limit of 60 per cent for the gold value of the dollar, and under its authority the President set the price of gold at $35 an ounce.

The gold-buying operation had incensed conservatives without appeasing the inflationists, especially the silverites. Silver had less economic significance than glue or strawberries or linoleum, but the cohesive bloc of silver senators from the mountain states wielded enough power to win concessions. In June 1934 Congress passed the Silver Purchase Act, which directed the Secretary of the Treasury to buy silver until it reached one fourth of the country's monetary reserve or until the world price of the metal climbed to $1.29 an ounce.

Secretary of Labor Frances Perkins was the first woman Cabinet member, but the President did not let that inhibit other department heads. Once when Secretary of the Navy Claude Swanson hesitated to tell a joke in her presence, Roosevelt quickly said: "Go ahead, Claude; she's dying to hear it."

Roosevelt hoped that his program of controlled inflation along with the AAA's subsidies to farmers would boost farm prices and, by thus restoring balance to the economy, bring about an early recovery. But many of his advisers thought that, important as the farm program was, it had to be coupled with a massive operation aimed at industrial revival. Tugwell and other planners wanted centralized direction of the economy; businessmen wanted government authorization for trade associations to draft agreements; labor leaders sought to win commitments which would protect workers from exploitation. Roosevelt told the advocates of the various proposals to lock themselves up in a room and not to come out until they had agreed on a bill. In this fashion he secured an omnibus measure which Congress, with great trepidation, enacted.

This keystone of the New Deal's recovery program was the National Industrial Recovery Act. Adopted in June 1933, it authorized business to draft industry-wide agreements exempt from the antitrust laws. Section 7(a) guaranteed workers the right to collective bargaining and stipulated that the agreements, called "codes," should set minimum wages and maximum hours. The act also provided for $3.3 billion in public works. In the House debate Representative James M. Beck charged that men like Moley, Tugwell and Berle, "fresh from the academic cloisters of Columbia University and with the added inspiration of all they have learned in Moscow," were attempting to undo the work of the founding fathers. But many businessmen, including leaders of the U.S. Chamber of Commerce, approved the new departure.

To head the National Recovery Administration, or NRA, Roosevelt named Brigadier General Hugh Johnson, a pugnacious former United States Cavalry officer who flung himself into codemaking with an abandon that startled old government hands in Washington. In an era when few men flew, Johnson commandeered an Army plane and traveled all over the country, buttonholing businessmen, cajoling, arguing, getting them to sign codes. A colorful and articulate figure, Johnson often treated his opponents to choice invective. He attacked "perfumed guys from the State Department" and critics "in whose veins there must flow something more than a trace of rodent blood."

Secretary of State Cordell Hull was a Tennessee mountaineer with a reputation for integrity. There is a story that as a back-country judge he told some spectators to stop sitting on the courtroom window sills. When one man refused, Hull promptly fined him for contempt. The man was his own father.

WE DO OUR PART

The famous Blue Eagle (above) calls on everyone to do his part under the National Recovery Administration. The emblem was displayed everywhere, including the sunburned backs of starlets Frances Drake (below, left) and Toby Wing. In New York City 250,000 marched in an NRA parade while 1.5 million watched; it cost the city $5,000 just to clean up afterward.

To dramatize the campaign for the NRA, Johnson created the symbol of a blue eagle with the legend "We Do Our Part." The Blue Eagle was based on the thunderbird, an ancient American Indian ideograph, which Johnson sketched on paper after hearing about it from Henry Wallace. Overnight, the NRA eagle appeared everywhere—on newspaper front pages, in store windows, even on the costumes of girls in the chorus. In Philadelphia a socialite named Bert Bell paid his respects to the NRA by dubbing his new professional football team the "Eagles."

To enforce the Blue Eagle, Johnson rallied the women of the country, urging them to shop only for merchandise made under an NRA code. "It is zero hour for housewives," he declared. "Their battle cry is 'Buy now under the Blue Eagle.' " By mid-September Johnson had won the nation's 10 biggest industries to NRA codes.

IN the next two years the National Recovery Administration chalked up some impressive achievements. It provided jobs for workers, it established a national pattern of maximum hours and minimum wages, it outlawed child labor and all but wiped out the sweatshop. But some corporations used their powers under the codes to stifle competition, boost prices and cut back production. As a consequence, progress toward recovery was painfully slow.

Yet the weakness of the early New Deal lay less in the NRA than in the absence of any consistent strategy to boost either purchasing power or investment. The framers of the Recovery Act had hoped that the $3.3 billion appropriation for public works would be an important lever for industrial recovery. But Roosevelt was skeptical of the value of public works and did not hesitate to raid the grant to get money for other projects.

Secretary of the Interior Harold Ickes, who administered the program, operated so cautiously that the Public Works Administration did next to nothing to stimulate the economy. Ickes, worried about the possibility of graft, insisted on reviewing every word of every PWA contract. The hard-working, sardonic secretary won himself the sobriquet of "Honest Harold," but neither he nor the President showed much understanding of the economic significance of public works.

Despite its lack of boldness, the PWA changed the face of the land. It built highways, power plants, hospitals, schools; it constructed or helped construct such mammoth dams as Fort Peck in Montana; it put up housing projects; it helped build Chicago's subway and it helped modernize the armed services by using its funds for new facilities and equipment.

Strictly as engines of recovery, however, other agencies were more important—notably the Reconstruction Finance Corporation. Created in January 1932, the RFC had been administered so timidly by Hoover's appointees that it frustrated the intent of Congress, which was to revitalize the economy. Roosevelt named as the agency's new head the Texas banker Jesse Jones. Under his vigorous leadership the RFC became not only the nation's largest bank but its biggest single investor.

Roosevelt's actions in his first two weeks in office represented his response to the immediate crisis. The constellation of recovery acts and edicts—AAA, controlled inflation, NRA, PWA, RFC—constituted his program to fight the Depression. But even in his first weeks in office, the new President was turning his attention to a third aim: deep-rooted reform of the nation's financial system to insure that such a crisis would never be repeated. On March 29, Roosevelt asked Congress for federal supervision of securities.

Debate on the bill took place while a Senate committee summoned J. P. Morgan Jr. and others to the stand. The committee's revelation of malpractices on Wall Street heightened the popular outcry for disciplinary action. The Securities Act, adopted in late May, provided for government supervision of the issue of new securities, required each new issue to be accompanied by a statement of financial information and made company directors civilly and criminally liable for misinformation.

In February 1934 Roosevelt asked Congress for legislation to regulate stock exchanges. Richard Whitney, president of the New York Stock Exchange, led the attack on the measure. "I think this bill is almost a full brother to the prohibition law," Whitney argued. "This matter involves human nature. You can't stop a man from taking a drink by passing a law prohibiting it. And any attempt to regulate by statute and in minute detail the operation of security markets is just as impossible of accomplishment."

Whitney organized the nation's stockbrokers to inundate Washington with letters and wires denouncing the bill. But Roosevelt outmaneuvered him. He achieved an entente with Wall Street moderates who represented stock-exchange firms that distrusted Whitney's leadership, and with out-of-town exchanges that were less insular and more sensitive to the popular demand for regulation. On June 6, 1934, the President signed the act creating the Securities and Exchange Commission (SEC). In later years, as none of the horrors Whitney had predicted came to pass, his influence on the exchange grew less; by the time he was caught embezzling and sentenced to prison in 1938, the old Wall Street crowd was finished.

Cupid proposes a "code for marriage recovery" in this cartoon, published at a time when many young people felt they could not afford to wed. Such a code was not so farfetched. Within a year after NRA's inception, it had organized under codes approximately 96 per cent of American industry and commerce, covering products from autos to chewing gum.

B Y the spring of 1934 the country had pulled out of the depths of the Depression. Construction for the first quarter of the year was up 136 per cent over the first quarter of 1933, steel output was up 132 per cent. Orders for merchandise were pouring into Chicago, headquarters of the nation's mail-order business. The New York Telephone Company was installing thousands of new phones, and it was hard to find a seat on Manhattan subway trains bound for the financial district. Traveling through the South that spring, reporter Rud Rennie was astonished at the change. Brass bands met the touring New York Giants at every railroad station, Mel Ott and Bill Terry and Carl Hubbell were paraded through the streets, people elbowed their way into ball parks. Signs of New Deal projects dotted the landscape, hotels opened entire floors that had been vacant, smoke billowed from chimneys that had been unused a year before.

In a year's time Franklin Roosevelt and the New Deal had enacted more significant social and economic legislation than had been passed in all of America's previous history. The government was spending millions to support farmers, was engaged in an unprecedented program of industry-government co-operation, had undertaken massive public works spending, had sanctioned the unionization of industrial America, had guaranteed the small-bank deposits of the country and had established federal regulation of Wall Street. The nation still had a long way to go, but it had a vigor and a sense of purpose that had seemed almost beyond expectation only 12 short months before.

MILITARISM ABROAD is attacked by George Grosz in a merciless painting which portrays one Nazi soldier as an obese brute and two others as emaciated fanatics. A native of Germany, Grosz continued waging war on Nazism after he came to America.

An art of protest in a troubled era

WHILE art has always reflected the period in which it was created, no art has been addressed more explicitly to its time than American works of social realism in the '30s. The painters of those years not only recorded what they saw; they engaged their art in causes about which they had strong feelings—the struggle of unions for recognition, the search of the unemployed for jobs, the yearning of the dispossessed for social and political changes. Artists of every kind joined the battle. There were Communists and non-Communists. There were established artists such as Max Weber, who captured the despair of job seekers, and newcomers such as Fletcher Martin, who painted labor violence with the authority of an ex-sailor and migrant worker. There were caricaturists such as William Gropper, who slashed at politicians with satire. The government encouraged artists on an unprecedented scale, commissioning their work for public buildings and putting them on salary—at a top pay of $94.90 a month—in the Federal Art Project of the WPA.

Deep concern over the crucial problems of the day is evident in works as dissimilar as the Reginald Marsh tempera painting shown opposite and the George Grosz watercolor which appears above. Marsh compassionately portrayed the problems of life in the big city. Grosz, a German who was denounced by Hitler and whose books were burned in his homeland, immigrated to the United States in 1932. "When I came to America, I came into power," he declared. "America is the only place I know where man can really be free."

UNEMPLOYMENT AT HOME brings despair to a group of home-less men in *The Park Bench* by Reginald Marsh. Painted in 1933, it reflects a period when public places in every city were filled with idle men who often had nowhere else to go. Dur-ing the late '30s, the Communist *Daily Worker*, which one of these men is reading, reached its peak circulation of 100,000.

The human backwash of economic disaster

No one knew exactly how many people were out of work during the Depression: A complete count was never made, and estimates ranged anywhere from 12 million to 16 million. But casual observation was enough to show that the jobless rate was appallingly high. The sight of men waiting forlornly for work or clustering in bread lines struck a responsive chord in the nation's artists, many of whom were personally acquainted with poverty. Max Weber, for example, was an immigrant whose father had reared him in Brooklyn on a tailor's income. As a youth Weber lived for three years on $2,000 while he studied in Paris with Matisse and visited the museums of Europe. In 1938 Weber expressed his deep concern about the Depression in the eloquent canvas *Seeking Work (opposite, top)*.

About half of all the American jobless were concentrated in the nation's large cities, and it was here that the artists of social protest found their greatest inspiration. Isaac Soyer's grim *Employment Agency (opposite)* was described in the New York *Sun* in 1937 as the "best of the pictures devoted to the New York life of the moment." For many it was a period of bleak despair.

THE HELPLESS gather before a factory in Max Weber's *Seeking Work*. The men seen at the left gesticulate heavenward, as if imploring or expecting divine assistance. The painting was one of Weber's favorites, and he never offered it for sale.

THE HOMELESS cluster in a "hobo jungle" on New York's Lower East Side in this painting by Reginald Marsh. Because many such jungles lacked sanitation, the police were often required to clear out the area and put the hobos back on the road.

THE JOBLESS dejectedly wait for a work call in Isaac Soyer's *Employment Agency*. Unemployment struck at all classes. In 1937, the year that this picture was painted, it was estimated that less than half of all the men out of work were unskilled.

STRIKING WORKERS in a picture by Ben Shahn wait out a 1937 strike at a Republic Steel plant in Warren, Ohio. At right is their ironic sign "welcoming" strikebreakers. The strikers ultimately went back to work without a union contract.

A graphic record of labor's clash with management

IN the '30s, artists of widely divergent backgrounds were in the thick of the labor strife, and they unflinchingly depicted what they saw. Fletcher Martin was a self-taught painter who had been a seaman, boxer and farm hand. "I am an American product," he said. "What the hell else would I paint but the things about western America that I have seen and know?"

Ben Shahn had received sound formal training in art. Brought to America as a boy and raised in a Brooklyn tenement, he became an apprentice lithographer at 15.

During the Depression he worked for a while as an artist and photographer for the Farm Security Administration. He painted *Scabbies Are Welcome (opposite)* during the CIO's unsuccessful Little Steel strike in 1937.

Philip Evergood, whose *American Tragedy* appears below at the left, was educated at Eton and Cambridge. But, he said, "I wasn't fitted for that academic rah-rah stuff." His biting satires of social evils and his sympathetic paintings of the workers' plight won him praise as a man who "concerns himself with human injustice."

FIGHTING ON THE DOCKS, a striker and a strikebreaker battle it out in *Trouble in Frisco, 1938,* part of a Fletcher Martin painting in New York's Museum of Modern Art. During the '30s violence often flared on the San Francisco waterfront.

BREAKING UP A MEETING, South Chicago police use guns and clubs on strikers and their families on Memorial Day, 1937. Philip Evergood's painting shows the height of the clash, in which 10 died and scores were hurt.

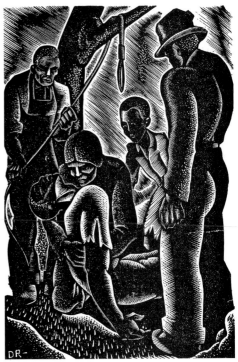

LYNCHED, a Negro victim of racists is cradled by a mourner in this woodcut by Dan Rico. It was estimated that lynchings occurred in 1935 at a rate of one in three weeks.

More misery for an oppressed minority

No American group suffered more acutely during the Depression than did the Negroes. The first to lose their jobs, they were subjected to increased humiliation and sporadic violence (above). Artist Alexander Brook, who did the painting shown at left during a trip South in 1939, was appalled by what he saw there. "I suppose unconsciously I reflected that in my painting," he commented later, "although I wasn't trying to put over any message. I think there is something in *Georgia Jungle* of the squalor which struck me as being so unbelievable existing right in the heart of America."

SMUGLY PROUD of their ancestors, these three women in Grant Wood's painting *Daughters of Revolution* put their trust in the past. Wood did not expect a purely American culture "until the whole colonial idea is put in the museum where it belongs."

SLYLY PEERING through a right-angle viewfinder, artist Ben Shahn (*extreme left*) snaps a picture of self-righteous parishioners in his 1939 painting, *Self Portrait among Churchgoers*. Many Shahn works during the '30s were commissioned by the WPA.

Critics of complacency, champions of reform

THE artists of the '30s went far beyond simple protest against the hardships of the time. Grant Wood felt that America had failed to create an original national culture. This he blamed on the stultifying influence of the past, and in the work reproduced above he satirized the smug upholders of colonial traditions. Reginald Marsh clearly revealed his distaste for sham in portraying rich operagoers (*right*). He said, "I'd rather paint an old suit of clothes than a new one, because an old one has character, reality is exposed and not disguised. People of wealth spend money to disguise themselves." Ben Shahn, under fire for a new mural in 1938, denied charges that the work was "irreligious"—and spoofed his attackers in the painting shown opposite.

CONCEITEDLY PREENING, wealthy box holders survey an opera audience in this detail from *Monday Night at the Metropolitan*, painted by Reginald Marsh in 1936. Obviously these patrons of the arts came to be seen, and they were not at all impatient for the performance to start.

THREE CORRUPT MEN—a policeman, a politician and a banker —are mercilessly portrayed in this detail of a Levine painting done for the WPA, now at New York's Museum of Modern Art.

Slashing attacks
on the abusers of power

THERE was an intensity to political feeling in the '30s that was something new for most Americans. Never before had the government involved itself so intimately in the lives of so many people. The Depression created doubts about the American system of free enterprise, making many people receptive to sweeping criticism of the old order.

Social and political protest filled the paintings of savage satirists like Jack Levine and William Gropper. Levine, whose *Feast of Pure Reason* appears above, felt that a painter should follow his natural bent, and that his own art was "equipped to punish." Grafters and charlatans are treated with contempt in his paintings, and he said, "Those I love, I simply leave out." Gropper, who painted *The Opposition (right)*, was compared to Daumier for his trenchant comments on all kinds of injustice. Also like Daumier, he came to painting from an influential career as a political cartoonist.

As the Depression relaxed its grip, the bitterness of American artists ebbed. By the mid-'40s, their art of protest had all but disappeared from the American scene.

Blocking progress, a legislator waves a sheaf of blank paper in

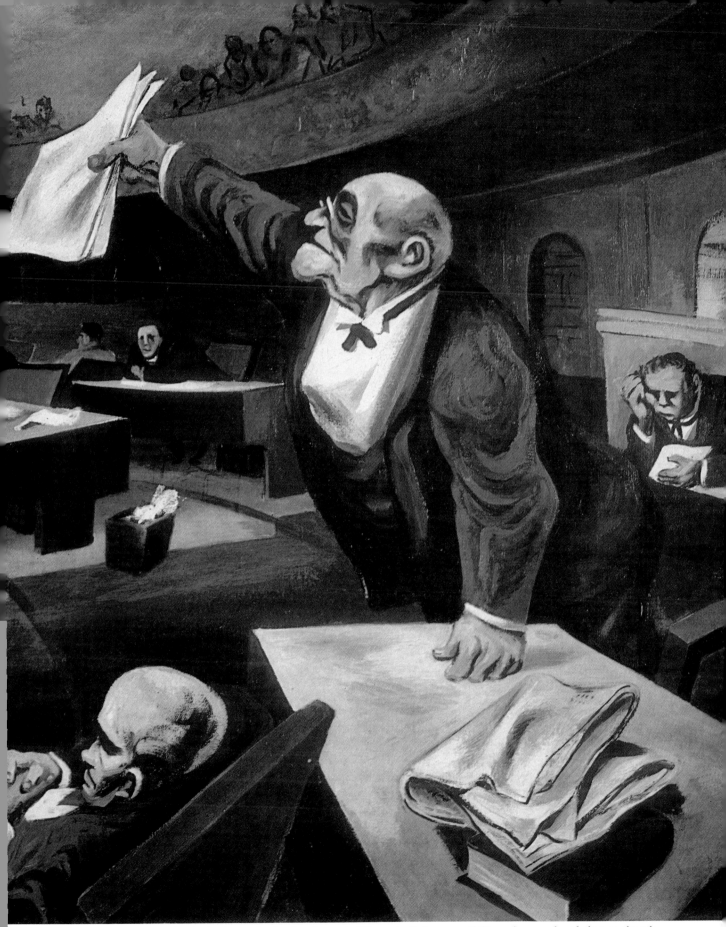

this William Gropper canvas. In the background other legislators, indifferent to their responsibilities, doze, read and chat on the job.

27

2. ENTER THE WELFARE STATE

IN the spring of 1934 the surge toward recovery began to falter. Indicators of business activity fell; the iron and steel trade went into the doldrums once again. By fall industrial employment was about as badly off as it had been a year before; in December New York City reported nearly one fourth of its population on relief. Suddenly the Roosevelt touch no longer seemed to be working.

Amid the discontent of that year a spirit of radicalism became clearly apparent in the nation. New political prophets arose to challenge the New Deal with panaceas of their own. The churning labor movement turned to more dynamic leaders. Men in Congress and the Administration began pressing stronger solutions to the nation's problems. Between them, the twin forces of the radical unrest and the President's own desire for more fundamental reforms would give birth by mid-1935 to a new phenomenon in America: the welfare state.

Of all Roosevelt's political challengers, the most troublesome was Louisiana's Senator Huey P. Long Jr. After establishing a benevolent tyranny as governor of his native state, Long had arrived in Washington in 1932 with a plan to divide the nation's riches among all the people. Long's Share-Our-Wealth organization attracted millions. A Chicago shoe salesman wrote him: "I voted for Pres. Roosevelt but it seems Wall St. has got him punch drunk. What we need is men with guts to go farther to the left as you advocate." A national poll indicated Long might win four million votes on a third-party ticket in 1936.

Almost as threatening to Roosevelt's command of the forces of reform was

A VICTIM OF DUST STORMS, a farmer ponders his devastated fields. Ben Shahn's lithograph publicized efforts of government agencies to aid impoverished families.

Detroit's "Radio Priest," Father Charles E. Coughlin, who commanded a national audience estimated at up to 45 million weekly. An isolationist, Coughlin also had a program for financial reform; his assaults on the "international bankers" had anti-Semitic implications which became clearer year by year.

The third of the Pied Pipers who challenged the President was Dr. Francis E. Townsend, sponsor of a proposal to pay people over 60 a pension of $200 a month. Critics pointed out that this would mean spending more than half the nation's income to compensate 9 per cent of the people. But Townsend stubbornly claimed that his plan would not only help old people but would restore prosperity. By the end of 1935 Townsend forces controlled the politics of several Western states. If Townsend, Long and Coughlin could unite in 1936, they might spell serious trouble for Roosevelt and the New Dealers.

THE same spirit of discontent on which Townsend, Long and Coughlin fed triggered a new interest in industrial unionism. In the summer of 1933 John L. Lewis launched an organizing drive in the coal fields which shot the membership of his United Mine Workers from 150,000 to more than 500,000 in a single year. All over America industrial workers rushed to join unions.

The American Federation of Labor, primarily a craft-union organization, found this influx of industrial workers an embarrassment. In Akron more than 60,000 rubber workers organized, and AFL leaders divided them among seven different craft unions. By the spring of 1935 they had all but vanished from the federation's rolls. Of 100,000 steel-union recruits who signed up in 1933 and 1934, only 5,300 were still paying dues in late 1934. Men who had joined the unions in high hopes were now tearing up their union cards in disgust.

Late in 1934 insurgent AFL leaders demanded that the federation conduct a vigorous drive to organize factory workers. These advocates of industrial unionism came to the Atlantic City convention in October 1935 determined on a showdown. Near the end of an uproarious meeting, there occurred a historic encounter between Lewis and "Big Bill" Hutcheson of the Carpenters, representing the craft interests. Hutcheson cursed Lewis, Lewis knocked Hutcheson down and both fell to the floor fighting. No amount of oratory could have reflected more clearly the irrevocable break between the new and the old.

Three weeks later Lewis and a group of supporters set up a Committee for Industrial Organization (CIO), which was ultimately to split away from the federation, changing its name to the *Congress* of Industrial Organizations.

It was a restless, growing, uneasy period for American labor. In 1934 the country was shaken by a series of violent strikes, many of them led by avowed radicals. After a rally addressed by Socialist leader Norman Thomas, 4,000 striking taxi drivers and their sympathizers marched into the center of Philadelphia hurling stones, battling and disarming policemen and overturning and burning taxicabs. In Wisconsin a strike against the Milwaukee Electric Railway and Light Company, supported by thousands of recruits from an organization of the unemployed largely controlled by the Socialists, threatened to paralyze the southeast corner of the state. The company, helpless, signed a settlement which recognized the unions and granted their demands. A textile walkout, the greatest strike in the history of the country up to that time, hit mills from New England to the Deep South. A strike of truckers in Minneapolis aimed to tie up the entire transportation system of that open-shop stronghold. In a pitched battle between strikers and deputized businessmen, fought

A cartoon decries the bitterness of labor disputes of the '30s. Both unions and management frequently resorted to violence. A Senate committee reported that 282 companies spent $9.4 million for munitions, spies and strikebreakers from 1933 to 1937; General Motors' share was a million dollars. Republic Steel was called the largest buyer of tear gas in the country.

before a fascinated crowd of 20,000, two men died and scores were injured.

The most dramatic strike of all—the San Francisco general strike of 1934—sprang out of the attempt of the International Longshoremen's Association to organize the West Coast waterfront. When the employers refused to recognize the ILA, the longshoremen struck. For two months cargoes of steel and perishables piled up on docks and in warehouses from San Diego to Vancouver.

In early July, with the strike almost two months old and no settlement in sight, industry leaders decided to open the port of San Francisco by force. On July 5, "Bloody Thursday," the Embarcadero was an avenue of violence. For hours strikers and police battled for control. Two strikers were killed; many on both sides were injured. Bloody Thursday infuriated San Francisco workers. The local Communist party called for a general strike. Even old-line conservative unions joined the movement. On July 16 pickets blockaded highways and barred incoming trucks. Tailors, barber shops, laundries, theaters, gas stations and other shops were shut down tight. Civic and business leaders panicked. In Washington Secretary of Labor Frances Perkins discovered Secretary of State Cordell Hull and Attorney General Homer Cummings poring over the *Encyclopaedia Britannica* to see whether the West Coast walkout met the definition of a "general strike." Miss Perkins sanely viewed the episode not as a real general strike but as a spontaneous move to win the right to union recognition. Walter Lippmann agreed: "What we see is a revolutionary weapon being wielded by men who do not want revolution." After a few hours the strike began to crumble; on the fourth day it was called off.

Women, too, participated in the labor-management struggles of 1935. The garment workers above displayed their posters during a walkout that affected 10,000 workers. Others made more dramatic gestures. To show sympathy with striking clerks, Mary Slate (below) had herself chained to a New York City lamppost. Police, unmoved, sawed her loose and sent her home.

THE same quasi-radical temper which characterized the San Francisco general strike and the other labor outbursts that year was reflected in the 1934 elections. In California the socialist novelist Upton Sinclair ran for governor under the slogan "End Poverty in California," easily won the Democratic primary and gave Republican Frank F. Merriam a bad scare before succumbing in the November election. Elsewhere in the country most Republicans looked forward to the 1934 elections with high hopes. The party in power traditionally loses a substantial number of congressional seats in a mid-term election, and there were predictions that the G.O.P. would gain up to 50 House seats. Not all Republican leaders were that optimistic; nevertheless, the party ran an adamantly conservative campaign. What the country needed, Ogden Mills declared, was another President like William McKinley.

The election results were a rude surprise. The Republicans *lost* 14 House seats; in the Senate the Old Guard was virtually wiped out. If the elections revealed anything, it was that a good part of the country was actually well to the left of the New Deal. The reformist mood of the nation and the political mandate of the election brought rejoicing to reform-minded New Dealers. "Boys—this is our hour," Roosevelt aide Harry Hopkins exulted. "We've got to get everything we want—a works program, social security, wages and hours, everything—now or never."

Roosevelt, also persuaded of the need for further reforms, turned first to overhauling his relief operations. Two months after he took office he had initiated a massive relief program, administered through state and local agencies. To head the new Federal Emergency Relief Administration, Roosevelt named Hopkins, a dynamic New York social worker. Hopkins went straight to the RFC building and, without even waiting for his desk to be installed, spent five million dollars in the next two hours, working among discarded packing cases.

But the FERA program left much to be desired. People on direct relief felt humiliated. Applying for assistance was like making a formal admission of inadequacy. The applicant's esteem suffered another blow when an investigator entered his home to ascertain whether his application was truthful. Relief recipients were often too proud to go to the depot to accept surplus commodities lest they be recognized. One New York small businessman, determined to hold to the values he had learned, insisted on paying his rent regularly, even at the sacrifice of the family's food. The government, after learning how little the family spent for food, cut off the relief altogether, suspecting fraud.

When it became evident that the FERA would be inadequate to carry the country over the winter of 1933-1934, Hopkins persuaded Roosevelt to try a different approach. The result was the Civil Works Administration, a strictly federal operation which paid not a relief stipend but minimum wages. In two months Hopkins invented jobs for four million men and women.

By the mid-'30s some observers felt the government was so committed to vast public-works programs like CWA that it could not let go even if it wanted to (above). Sure enough, after CWA ended, it was eventually replaced by the even more expensive WPA, which prompted the cartoon seen below. The caption said: "They don't come any bigger than me, buddy."

THE CWA was a godsend to millions. Frank Walker, the head of the President's National Emergency Council, investigated reports of wasteful CWA activities in his home state of Montana and returned a convinced supporter of the agency. "I saw old friends of mine—men I had been to school with—digging ditches and laying sewer pipe. They were wearing their regular business suits as they worked because they couldn't afford overalls and rubber boots." One of Walker's friends pulled out some silver coins and said: "Do you know, Frank, this is the first money I've had in my pockets in a year and a half?"

In its brief span, the CWA built or improved some 255,000 miles of roads, 30,000 schools, more than 3,700 playgrounds and athletic fields, and a thousand airports. The agency fought the citrus canker in Texas, the gypsy moth in New England and the sweet-potato weevil in the South. Republican Governor Alfred Landon of Kansas wrote the President: "This civil-works program is one of the soundest, most constructive policies of your administration, and I cannot urge too strongly its continuance."

Nevertheless, Roosevelt decided to terminate the CWA by the spring of 1934. He was alarmed at its cost, and there appeared to be local graft involved in its operation. Despite widespread protest, the agency was closed down, and the country returned to direct relief. By the end of 1934 more than 20 million Americans—one out of every six—were receiving public assistance.

But Roosevelt and Hopkins still believed that disbursing money to able-bodied men and asking nothing in return was bound to damage their self-respect. Early in 1935 the President asked Congress for an ambitious work relief program to give jobs to 3.5 million unemployed. The resultant Emergency Relief Appropriation Act of 1935 authorized the greatest single appropriation of its kind in human history: nearly five billion dollars.

To spend this huge grant, Roosevelt created a Works Progress Administration, and once more called on Harry Hopkins to administer it. Under Hopkins the WPA built a vast number of public works: hospitals, schools, airports and playgrounds. It controlled crickets in Wyoming, planted eight million bushels of oysters in oyster beds and gave Oklahoma City's zoo a monkey pen.

The WPA found ingenious ways of putting people to work. A young writer named John Steinbeck was told to take a census of all the dogs on Monterey Peninsula in California. Other creative men were given assignments more in keeping with their talents. With WPA funds the Federal Theatre brought O'Neill and Shaw to Iowa farming villages and enabled New Yorkers, at a top price of 55 cents, to see T. S. Eliot's *Murder in the Cathedral*. In four years WPA productions were seen by some 30 million people.

The Federal Writers' Project gave opportunities to many new writers—among them John Cheever and Richard Wright—as well as to established ones, including Conrad Aiken. The project turned out about a thousand publications including some 50 state and territorial guides, 30 city guides and 20 regional guides. The state guides scored an unanticipated commercial success; the one on Massachusetts sold 8,000 copies in the first month.

In 1935 some 18,000 musicians were on the relief rolls. The WPA's Federal Music Project employed 15,000 of them. The standard of quality was generally high: Three WPA orchestras—the Buffalo Philharmonic, the Oklahoma City Symphony and the Utah Symphony—later developed into established ensembles. "Nowhere in Europe," declared the Austrian composer Erich Wolfgang Korngold, "is there anything that even compares with it."

The Federal Art Project employed both artists of modest talents and many major painters including Stuart Davis, Jackson Pollock and Yasuo Kuniyoshi. It sponsored an *Index of American Design* which had a considerable impact; the Shaker furniture shown in it influenced modern furniture designers, and Pennsylvania Dutch pottery inspired commercial designers of dishware.

Millions of young men and women who had come of working age during the Depression had never held a job. The National Youth Administration (NYA) aimed to keep them off home relief rolls and either train them in job skills or help them to stay in school. In eight years the NYA gave part-time employment to more than 600,000 college students, 1.5 million high school pupils, and 2.5 million youngsters who were no longer in school. NYA workers built a roadside park along Minnesota's Saint Croix River, renovated the Pawtucket Boys' Club in Rhode Island and cleaned test tubes in university laboratories.

Novelist Upton Sinclair was almost elected governor of California in 1934, when he ran on his EPIC (End Poverty in California) program. Later he remarked that if he had won the race he might have lost his life; a businessman "had made out his will, got a revolver. . . . If I had won, he was going to shoot me." Sinclair said thoughtfully: "I'm glad I wasn't elected."

BUT the most popular of all the New Deal works agencies was the Civilian Conservation Corps. The CCC put a total of 2.5 million young men to work in the forests, living under Army supervision. They fed wildlife, counted game, battled Dutch elm disease, cleared beaches and camping grounds, built fish ponds and fought forest fires; in this last activity 47 CCC men lost their lives. Most of all they planted trees; of all the forest planting, public and private, in the nation's first 175 years, more than half was done by the CCC.

The work of the CCC reflected one of the major goals of the New Deal: conservation of the land. The terrible drought of the early 1930s, coupled with decades of misguided land practices, converted a huge area from Texas to the Dakotas into a "Dust Bowl." Year after year the dust storms came, casting an ominous black pall that turned noon into midnight on the Great Plains. In Austin, Texas, legislators donned surgical masks; in Western hospitals children suffering from pneumonia gasped under wet cloths. Dust from Nebraska fell on the Atlantic Seaboard; in Boston dust almost blotted out the sun. In 1935 Congress created the Soil Conservation Service, with orders to seek solutions to the problems of soil erosion. The Soil Conservation and Domestic Allotment Act, adopted the following year, authorized federal payments to farmers who engaged in practices recommended by the Conservation Service.

The most dazzling success of the New Deal conservationists was the crea-

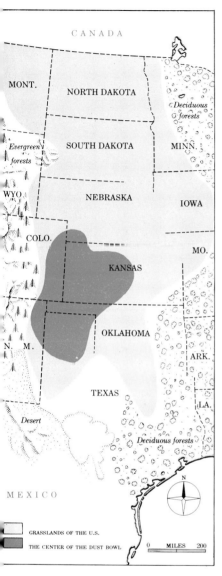

THE DUST BOWL:

DISASTER ON THE PLAINS

The Dust Bowl of the '30s began in Kansas, in a part of the Great Plains that had always known dust. Following a severe drought in 1933, a series of dust storms swept the region. In one of these in April of 1935, flying gravel derailed a locomotive, broke store windows and damaged almost $20 million worth of wheat in the Texas Panhandle alone. At that point families began to move out; the term "Dust Bowl" was coined to describe the ravaged region (dark brown), which ultimately cut into Kansas, Nebraska, New Mexico, Colorado, Oklahoma and Texas.

tion of the Tennessee Valley Authority in 1933. For years progressives in Congress, led by Senator George Norris of Nebraska, had fought for public development of the electric power and nitrogen complex built during World War I at Muscle Shoals on the Tennessee River. Twice Congress had passed a Muscle Shoals bill; twice Republican Presidents had vetoed it. The new Democratic President proposed not only hydroelectric power development, but a vast regional experiment in social planning, conservation and unified development of the resources of the valley.

Utility company executives exploded. "I can see no market whatever for this power," announced the Southern tycoon E. A. Yates. Private power executives protested that TVA was socialism and that it had unfair advantages in competing with privately owned firms. But TVA more than justified the development hopes held out for it. It brought electricity to a valley where in 1933 only two out of every 100 farms had light and power. It built multipurpose dams which served as reservoirs to control floods and at the same time generated cheap, abundant hydroelectric power. TVA manufactured fertilizer, dug a 650-mile navigation channel from Knoxville to Paducah, engaged in soil conservation and reforestation, and co-operated with state and local agencies in rural planning. It gave new life to the entire region's economy.

TVA was only one of a number of major public-power developments initiated by the New Deal. In the Pacific Northwest the government erected mighty Bonneville Dam on the Columbia River and, in eastern Washington, mammoth Grand Coulee Dam, the greatest concrete structure in the world, which backed up water into a lake 150 miles long.

It was not only Tennessee and the West that got cheap power under Roosevelt. When he took office nine out of 10 American farms had no electricity at all. The creation of the Rural Electrification Administration in 1935 did more than any other act of the decade to change the nation's rural life. The REA lent money to nonprofit co-operatives which strung lines into the countryside and which, by their example, goaded the utilities to undertake needed construction. By 1950 nine out of every 10 American farms had electricity.

ROOSEVELT'S bold move into the public-power field reflected widespread dissatisfaction with the operations of the private utilities in the 1920s. A Federal Trade Commission probe had revealed that many utility magnates had milked operating companies to amass profits for holding-company empires, had invaded the schoolroom by paying fees to teachers and by subsidizing slanted textbooks, and had corrupted members of legislatures. Critics placed most of the blame on the holding companies, which could shift their operations from state to state and cover one improper investment by yet another issue of securities before state commissions could untangle the existing skein. "A holding company," remarked Will Rogers, "is a thing where you hand an accomplice the goods while the policeman searches you."

To meet this evil head-on, on March 12, 1935, Roosevelt sent a bluntly worded message to Congress. "Except where it is absolutely necessary to the continued functioning of a geographically integrated operating utility system, the utility holding company with its present powers must go," he said. He added: "I am against private socialism of concentrated private power as thoroughly as I am against governmental socialism."

An army of utility lobbyists stormed Capitol Hill. Their attempts to bring pressure on the legislators were so blatant that both houses of Congress launched investigations. The Senate committee, headed by Senator Hugo Black of Alabama, found that the power companies had spent at least $1.5 million to defeat the holding-company legislation—money which would be charged to operating expenses on electricity bills. There was also testimony about forged telegrams, burned evidence and a bribed congressman.

An aroused Congress passed the Public Utility Holding Company Act in August 1935. It leveled the holding-company pyramids and empowered the SEC to supervise their financial transactions.

THE Holding Company Act showed the rising influence of the 78-year-old Supreme Court justice Louis Brandeis, who opposed bigness in both business and government. Brandeis urged Roosevelt to take action that would break big business into small units.

Brandeis won a number of New Dealers to his way of thinking. The most important were Benjamin V. Cohen, a skillful legislative draftsman, and Thomas G. Corcoran, a clever political manipulator. By the summer of 1935 the team of Cohen and Corcoran was coming to replace the earlier New Deal brain trust under Raymond Moley.

The influence of the Brandeis group made its real impact during the summer of 1935. The President had bided his time while the Longs and Coughlins held the center of the stage. Then in June, when his political fortunes seemed to have struck bottom, he made his move. He suddenly confronted Congress with a far-reaching program of "must" legislation and insisted that it remain in session until every item was adopted. He got his wish. During the "Second Hundred Days" Congress erected the framework of the welfare state.

The opening gun of Roosevelt's new campaign was an explosive tax message. Existing laws, the President said, resulted in "an unjust concentration of wealth and economic power." To prevent the transmission of this wealth from generation to generation, he urged increased taxes on inheritances and, to balk evasion, the imposition of gift taxes. He advocated as well "a definite increase in the taxes now levied upon very great individual net incomes." Finally, noting that the smallest corporation paid the same rate on net profits as a corporation a thousand times its size, the President recommended a tax graduated according to the size of corporation income.

Conservatives were incensed. They had disliked many New Deal measures, but this proposal reached directly into the pockets of the well-to-do. And indeed, Roosevelt's tax message scarcely even claimed to be concerned with raising revenues; he was openly using taxation as a social instrument. One House member complained: "This is a hell raiser, not a revenue raiser."

After a summer of torrid debate, Congress enacted the Revenue Act of 1935. The law levied an excess profits tax; stepped up estate, gift and capital stock taxes, and increased the surtax to record rates. Despite the outcry over the law, however, it actually did very little to redistribute income; not until the war years was there any real action in this direction.

A week after Roosevelt sent his tax message, Congress passed the Wagner National Labor Relations Act. Many of its supporters viewed its enactment as a minor miracle. One commented: "We who believed in the Act were dizzy with watching a 200-to-1 shot come up from the outside."

The law was the outgrowth of two years of frustration over attempts to

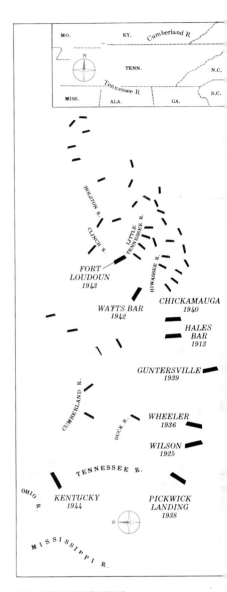

TVA: DOMESTICATING

A VAST RIVER SYSTEM

The Tennessee Valley Authority, an experiment in regional planning and rehabilitation, eventually operated a system of dams draining nearly 40,000 square miles and able to produce about four million kilowatts of electricity. The smaller dams held back flood waters in rainy seasons and, together with various locks, created a stable channel for navigation in the main stream. A few dams were built before TVA; some were privately owned. (In the large map, north is at left; the inset shows the same area with north at top and state borders added.)

For years certain conservatives remained vehement in their opposition to the Social Security Act of 1935. They claimed, among other things, that the act "depersonalized" beneficiaries and threatened individualism. Here the ordinary citizen is seen as a number in the eyes of the government, in a cartoon that underscores the increasing complexity of life in America.

give meaning to Section 7(a) of the National Industrial Recovery Act, which guaranteed workers the right of collective bargaining. Some businessmen had openly defied 7(a); others acknowledged its authority but circumvented its intent. Collective bargaining was all right, said the Minnesota businessman Charles L. Pillsbury, but "labor leaders have interpreted it to mean that collective bargaining can come only through belonging to a union."

When strikes threatened recovery, Roosevelt set up a National Labor Relations Board under Lloyd Garrison, Dean of the Wisconsin Law School, to solve labor disputes. The board, with little statutory power, was all but impotent by 1935. In the 33 noncompliance cases referred to the Attorney General between July 1, 1934, and March 1, 1935, not a single judgment was obtained.

Senator Robert F. Wagner of New York had drafted a bill in 1934 to give the board greater power, but it had been blocked by officials who feared that resultant strikes would impede attempts to achieve business recovery. Roosevelt himself was, as Moley remarked, a "patron" of labor who was more interested in what he could do for workers than in what labor could do for itself.

But when Wagner renewed his efforts in 1935, Roosevelt gave him the green light, though without enthusiasm and for reasons not wholly clear. Even more surprisingly, both houses of Congress approved the measure by wide margins. The National Labor Relations Act set up the NLRB as a permanent independent agency empowered not only to conduct elections to determine appropriate bargaining units and agents, but to restrain employers from committing "unfair labor practices" such as discharging workers for union membership or fostering employer-dominated company unions.

THE Wagner Act was not the only piece of New Deal legislation to be achieved more by the efforts of liberal senators than by Administration initiative. Wagner was also the sparkplug of the movement to achieve a federal housing act, another proposal Roosevelt viewed coolly at first. The plan also encountered, predictably, the hostility of the real-estate interests. But in 1937 Roosevelt swung his support to the measure, and this proved decisive. The act set up the United States Housing Authority and made available $500 million in loans for low-rent housing. The law marked the establishment of a new principle: federal responsibility for clearing slums and housing the poor.

Roosevelt's own housing program, put forward earlier, had centered on saving homeowners from foreclosure and encouraging home building under private auspices. In 1932 some 250,000 families had lost their homes. On the eve of Roosevelt's inauguration more than a thousand homes were being foreclosed every day. In June 1933 Congress created the Home Owners' Loan Corporation, which would help refinance one out of every five mortgaged urban private dwellings in America. A year later Congress set up the Federal Housing Administration, which insured loans made by private lending institutions to middle-income families to repair and modernize their homes or to build new ones. The HOLC and FHA saved the homes of thousands of Americans and enabled thousands more to buy houses of their own.

Though Roosevelt had relatively little interest in urban renewal, he was fascinated by schemes to remove slumdwellers to the countryside. In addition, Rexford Tugwell's Resettlement Administration hoped to move impoverished farmers from submarginal land and help them make a fresh beginning with modern tools and expert guidance. The New Deal built about 100 communities for such purposes. It also put up three "greenbelt" towns—new municipalities, frankly experimental, located close to employment and girdled by green countryside—near Washington, Cincinnati and Milwaukee.

Many questioned the wisdom of trying to resettle people in the country at a time when thousands of rural inhabitants were impoverished. Tractored off their land or blown out by the dust storms, migrant farmers had overrun the farm counties of the Pacific Coast, only to be drowned in a sea of cheap labor. Despite some minor federal efforts to help them, the sharecropper, the tenant farmer and the migrant remained America's neglected men.

OF all the measures enacted in the Second Hundred Days of 1935, the most symptomatic was the Social Security Act. Conservatives were aghast at Roosevelt's proposal for a comprehensive system of social insurance. "Social Security," insisted Herbert Hoover, "must be builded upon a cult of work, not a cult of leisure."

But most congressmen believed it was a program too long deferred. Decades earlier, countries like Germany and Great Britain had provided for security against the hazards of old age and joblessness in an industrial society. The Social Security Act of 1935 created a national system of old-age insurance, set up a federal-state program of unemployment insurance and provided federal aid to the states, on a matching basis, for care of dependent mothers and children, the crippled and the blind, and for public health services.

The Social Security Act reflected not only the humanitarianism of the 1930s but also the inclination of Americans in those years to seek security and group acceptance rather than self-realization and individual achievement. On the eve of the November 1936 election, President Roosevelt took note of the quest for security in explaining what his first term in office had signified:

"We have had to take our chance about our old age in days past. We have had to take our chances with depressions and boom times. We have had to take chances on our jobs. We have had to take chances on buying our homes.

"I have believed for a great many years that the time has come in our civilization when a great many of these chances should be eliminated from our lives. . . . I have felt that people in responsible positions . . . ought to make an effort, through legislation and through public opinion, in a perfectly normal, sane, sensible way, to provide security—security for people so that they would not individually worry, security for their families, security for their homes, a greater security for their jobs, and, incidentally, a greater security for the people who employ them."

Roosevelt had come a long way toward building the foundation for a welfare state. He had accepted responsibility for the welfare of millions of the unemployed; had pledged billions of dollars to save homes and farms from foreclosure; had engaged the government directly in clearing slums and building vast regional power developments; had underwritten the right to collective bargaining; had established a system of social security.

In his annual message to Congress in 1938, Roosevelt summed up his philosophy regarding welfare proposals: "Government has a final responsibility for the well-being of its citizenship. If private cooperative endeavor fails to provide work for willing hands and relief for the unfortunate, those suffering hardship from no fault of their own have a right to call upon the government for aid; and a government worthy of its name must make fitting response."

German-born Robert F. Wagner rose from poverty to become a leading New Deal senator and the sponsor of much enlightened social legislation. When a friend pointed out that Wagner's career proved that a modest beginning is no barrier to success, the senator snorted: "That is the most God-awful bunk. I came through it, yes. That was luck, luck, luck. Think of the others."

A tenant shack stands abandoned amidst tractor-made furrows in the Texas Panhandle. As tractors came in, men were pushed off the land.

Dark clouds for the U.S. farmer

FOR years the Great Plainsmen had misused the vast, open prairie lying between the Rockies and the Missouri-Mississippi waterway. They overgrazed the land with cattle and sheep, then put it to the plow and farmed it; they ripped off its protective grass matting so ruthlessly that a team of researchers examining the results years later reported: "The prairie sod is on the way to join the dodo." The high plains were semiarid and not really suitable for crops; they received only half the moisture of the Mississippi Valley. But World War I's two-dollar-a-bushel wheat and a spell of higher-than-average moisture encouraged over-zealous farmers. In 1923, for example, a single grower laid bare some 100,000 virgin acres.

The payoff came in the '30s. The sodbusting that had made the Great Plains the American breadbasket now led to the Dust Bowl. By late 1933 the area had been dry for 18 months, and there were dust storms from Oklahoma to South Dakota. In subsequent years the scalped land, dried to powder by drought, yielded to high winds; skies were black with wind-blown topsoil. One oldtimer said he could look out his window and count the Kansas farms going by. The number of farmers forced into tenancy increased at a rate of 40,000 a year. When even tenant farming did not pay, the banks and mortgage companies that had taken over the debt-ridden land sent in tractors, ripped aside fences, toppled tenant shacks and started mass cultivation. The farmers, broke, crammed into jalopies and headed for California—and fresh disaster.

A BROODING MOTHER feeds her child in an Oklahoma community camp in 1939. For four years her family had eked out a meager livelihood as migratory farm workers.

RISING WATERS of the Shenandoah River inundate a Virginia farm. In 1936, while thousands in the West were suffering from drought, farmers in the East were the victims of raging floods.

Nature's savage revenge on river and prairie

THE plundering of the land brought catastrophe to the East as well as to the West. Water could not be absorbed by the bare and burned slopes of devastated Eastern forests or the sod-denuded grasslands; rain and melting snow ran off fast, overflowing river banks. Along with the dust storms the nation suffered the greatest floods in its history. Much of Pittsburgh was inundated; the Potomac rose 26 feet at Washington and threatened government buildings; the Ohio took the lives of 900 people and drove 500,000 families from their homes.

In the West, meanwhile, winds lifted off 300 million tons of topsoil in a single day. Western farmers grew desperate. Their soil blown away, their shanties half buried in dust, the people slid downward with their impoverished land. In the '30s three of every five Oklahoma farmers were tenants; each year 40 per cent of these would break loose like tumbleweed and go rolling across the prairie until they lodged on some other, usually poorer, farm. In Kansas a farm wife wrote: "I could grovel on the ground sometimes. I feel so . . . beaten!"

FLYING DUST buffets an Oklahoma man and his sons outside a dune-mounded farm building. By 1935 wind storms had eroded nine million acres in the Great Plains alone.

Trundling all its earthly possessions, an Arkansas family plods through Memphis, Texas, some 500 miles from home, en route to the cotton

A girl waits in a battered car, California-bound. Children worked—when there was work.

A migrant mends a tire by a Southern road.

A Missourian, headed west, asks directions.

Migrants make a stop for repairs. United by common problems, they often moved in groups.

farms of the lower Rio Grande Valley. When migratory workers were too poor to own even jalopies, they simply traveled about on foot.

The great migration to a Western promised land

DUSTED out, flooded out, tractored out, the farmers resorted to the old American solution: They went west. They departed in confusion and bitterness. In John Steinbeck's *Grapes of Wrath*, the novel that made "Okies" a part of the American language and the American conscience, the despairing tenant, watching a tractor knock over his shack, asks, "Who can we shoot?" The driver, a local farmer, replies in bafflement: "Maybe there's nobody to shoot." In mounting numbers farmers began to leave the land. In 1936 in seven southeastern Colorado counties, half the houses were abandoned.

To California—in the words of historian Frederick Lewis Allen—"they came in decrepit, square-shouldered 1925 Dodges and 1927 LaSalles; in battered 1923 Model-T Fords that looked like relics of some antique culture . . . piled high with mattresses and cooking utensils and children, with suitcases, jugs and sacks strapped to the running boards." In four years 300,000 refugees were counted entering California by automobile. More than nine tenths were native American whites; a quarter came from Oklahoma, another quarter from Arkansas, Missouri and Texas. The women were sallow, the children gaunt. The stubble-faced men in their faded overalls looked puzzled and worried. When they spied a stranger they would stop their cars and say: "You think there's a chance farther up the valley? I need work bad."

FESTOONED WITH POSSESSIONS, an old auto heads west. At one time migrant traffic was so heavy that westbound cars jammed the roads from side to side, including eastbound lanes.

43

A pea picker's shanty in Imperial Valley, California (left), a migratory worker's hovel in Florida (center) and a Missouri sharecropper's

"We're bums and we've got to get out"

THE most shocking chapter of the Dust Bowl tragedy came when the refugees reached the promised land. They found an agriculture even more depersonalized than the one they had left, and joblessness too: When growers in one California town advertised for workers, they were flooded by three times as many people as there were jobs. Many Californians became apprehensive. In 1935 and 1936 the Los Angeles Chamber of Commerce tried—illegally and futilely—to turn back the migrants by a "Bum Blockade." "When they need us they call us migrants," said a grim farmer. "When we've picked their crops we're bums and we've got to get out."

The migrants cooked over campfires with water from irrigation ditches and lived in every conceivable kind of habitation. One investigator reported a two-room cabin in which 41 Okies slept. Wages depended on how many crop pickers showed up in answer to a call to work. If many appeared, hungry and anxious, they might work for as little as 45 cents a day; other days they might earn 45 cents an hour. Sporadically the Okies went on violent strikes and were met by tear gas, goon squads, espionage and vigilantes with pick handles.

In 1937 the U.S. Farm Security Administration moved in to help the migrants. At one time the FSA was supporting 30,000 families in California. In a difficult time this agency did much to alleviate the troubles of the migrants. But the problem was never really solved until the 1940s—when a war came along and swept the migrants out of the fields and into the booming factories.

A NEW HOME, built with FSA help, is proudly shown by a migrant's wife. Though only a shack, it was a vast improvement over the shanties most crop pickers lived in.

44

bedroom, where a small boy stands combing his hair (right), reflect the grim life that was led by thousands of poor farm families in the '30s.

THE·SWEATSHOP·AND·TENEMENT
OF·YESTERDAY·CAN·BE·THE·LI
ORDERED·WITH·JUSTICE·OF·TOMORRO

3. THE
ROOSEVELT
MAGIC

IN the 1930s the personality of Franklin D. Roosevelt was pervasive. He was a minor hero in Maxwell Anderson's musical *Knickerbocker Holiday*, he intervened in a comic strip to get Joe Palooka out of the French Foreign Legion, he was gently ribbed by George M. Cohan in the Broadway show *I'd Rather Be Right* ("Bring me another fireside," Cohan cried, "I'm going on the air"). Popular singers confided: "And Franklin Roosevelt's looks / Give me a thrill." In *Sing Out the News* a chorus chanted the praises of "Franklin D. Roosevelt Jones." Years later, professional football fans would cheer the appearance on the field of three mammoth players born in the '30s: Roosevelt Brown, Roosevelt Taylor and Roosevelt Grier.

Franklin Roosevelt dominated the front pages as no other President ever had. Yet few men claimed that they really knew him. It was as though the very burgeoning of publicized detail about the President's personal life—his stamp collection, his children, his Scotch terrier Fala—served to enlarge the public figure but obscure the man. Even to intimates Roosevelt rarely revealed his feelings. He kept his privacy hidden behind a mask of cheerful gregariousness.

"You are a wonderful person but you are one of the most difficult men to work with that I have ever known," Secretary of the Interior Ickes grumpily told the President one day.

"Because I get too hard at times?"

BETTER, FULLER LIFE under the New Deal is enjoyed this large family of erstwhile tenement dwellers George Biddle's mural, *Society Freed Through Justice*.

"No," said Ickes, "you never get too hard but you won't talk frankly even with people who are loyal to you and of whose loyalty you are fully convinced. You keep your cards close up against your belly."

Roosevelt's personal letters, the historian David Potter has noted, "are as unrevealing as the letters of George Washington. . . . For him a letter was an instrument of social communication, not of self-expression." Potter suggests, however, "this should not be taken to imply that Roosevelt hid his most intense thoughts. It is more probable, simply, that all his energies were turned outward, and that his life was one of action rather than of reflection." Not even the weightiest responsibilities of office seemed to disturb him. "He was like the fairy-story prince who didn't know how to shudder," wrote one of his advisers.

"You'll have to learn that public life takes a lot of sweat; but it doesn't need to worry you," Roosevelt once admonished his aide Rex Tugwell. "You won't always be right, but you mustn't suffer from being wrong. That's what kills people like us." He told his adviser that even a truck driver doing Tugwell's job would probably be right 50 per cent of the time; "but you aren't a truck driver. You've had some preparation. Your percentage is bound to be higher."

He was above all a practical man. He would try almost anything, as Frances Perkins has written, feeling that if it did not work it could be dropped with no harm done.

In one of his fireside chats, Roosevelt declared: "When Andrew Jackson, 'Old Hickory,' died, someone asked, 'Will he go to Heaven?' And the answer was, 'He will if he wants to.' If I am asked whether the American people will pull themselves out of this depression, I answer, 'They will if they want to.' . . . I have no sympathy with the professional economists who insist that things must run their course and that human agencies can have no influence on economic ills."

Franklin Roosevelt believed he belonged in the White House. He remembered seeing his "Uncle Ted" there, he had watched Woodrow Wilson from close range; the office seemed his almost as a birthright. As historian Richard Neustadt has observed: "Roosevelt, almost alone among our Presidents, had no conception of the office to live up to; he was it. His image of the office was himself-in-office." He loved the majesty of the position, relished its powers and rejoiced in the opportunity it offered for achievement. He never doubted he would measure up to the job. Franklin Roosevelt was, as he said of himself, "the least introspective man in the world," but he sensed that he had the right kind of mind and temperament for the particular office he felt himself destined to fill.

The actor George M. Cohan spoofs Franklin D. Roosevelt in the hit musical "I'd Rather Be Right." The show had F.D.R. admitting: "The trouble with this country is that I don't know what the trouble with the country is." In it, too, the Supreme Court—nine men, all resembling Chief Justice Charles Evans Hughes—declared everything unconstitutional but itself.

IT has become a commonplace, even among Roosevelt's admirers, to view the President as an intellectual lightweight. The fact is that Roosevelt was far better informed about economic matters—about utilities regulation, agriculture, banking, corporate structure, public finance—than he is generally credited with being. He was, to be sure, less well versed in economic theory—but that may have been just as well. Had he accepted the orthodox economic thinking of 1932 he would have been badly misguided.

Roosevelt was not a philosopher but a problem-solver. He had small talent for abstract reasoning; he read few books, and those not very seriously; he got his ideas from observation and from conversation. He loved brilliant people, noted one of his aides, but not profound ones. Raymond Moley, pointing out the difference between the two Roosevelts, once wrote that the picture of Theodore Roosevelt "regaling a group of his friends with judgments on Goya, Flaubert, Dickens, and Jung, and discussions of Louis the Fat or the number of men at arms seasick in the fleet of Medina Sidonia—this could never be mistaken for one of Franklin Roosevelt. F.D.R.'s interests have always been more circumscribed. His moments of relaxation are given over exclusively to simpler pleasures—to the stamp album, to the Currier and Ives naval prints, to a movie or to good-humored horseplay."

Yet almost everyone who worked with him was impressed by his knowledge of detail. The publisher J. David Stern recalled an occasion when the President recited the average price of 10 commodities for both 1933 and 1923 and was correct on 90 per cent of them. A stern critic of Roosevelt was flabbergasted during a conversation about judicial review to have the President quote long verbatim extracts from such abstruse works as James Madison's *Journal* and Jonathan Elliot's *Debates*. At one point TIME reported: "The President's particular forte is islands: he is said to know every one in the world, its peoples, habits, population, geography, economic life. When a ship sank off Scotland several months ago, experts argued: Had the ship hit a rock. . .? The President pondered latitude and longitude, said: 'It hit a rock. They ought to have seen that rock.' Naval aide Daniel J. Callaghan recalled the rock, disagreed. 'At high tide, Mr. President, that rock is submerged.' No such thing, said the President, even at high tide that rock is 20 feet out of water."

On the occasion of the Democrats' annual $100-a-plate Jackson Day Dinner, a cartoon depicts Jackson taking issue with the whole idea. F.D.R. liked to compare Jackson's troubles with his own. He once said: "It seemed sometimes that all were against him—all but the people of the United States." Then he added with great satisfaction: "History so often repeats itself."

MUCH attention has been given to the influence of Roosevelt's advisers in the creation of new programs. Actually, many of the more ingenious ideas of the New Deal were the President's own. He had a remarkably inventive mind which constantly devised fresh methods of approach. A typical example was the shelter belt—a proposal to help solve the dust-bowl problem by planting windbreaks of millions of trees in a 100-mile-wide strip across the nation from the Dakotas through Oklahoma. Opponents of the plan derided it—Governor "Alfalfa Bill" Murray of Oklahoma said it was "like trying to grow hair on a bald head"—but the President persisted. With WPA assistance the Forest Service planted more than 200 million trees in a broad band almost 1,000 miles long. Its success confounded the President's critics.

Roosevelt's love of experimentation brought the government into many strange new areas. Using federal relief funds, the documentary film maker Pare Lorentz ("What I want to do is photograph America—show the people what it really looks like") turned out the memorable "The Plow That Broke the Plains" in 1936 and the classic "The River" in 1937. With background music by Virgil Thomson, drawing upon American folk themes, these films dramatized man's mistreatment of the land.

The New Deal gave an unprecedented opportunity to university-trained experts. Men from the academic world had first appeared on the national stage in small numbers in the era of Theodore Roosevelt. During World War I they had had a brief moment of glory when they had been called to run the wartime agencies. But in the 1920s they had returned to the obscurity of their campuses. With Franklin Roosevelt's advent they emerged again—this time as members of a new elite: policy makers and administrators with the authority to impose their concepts of the national interest on economic institutions.

The capital had hitherto thought of government workers largely as civil service employees awaiting the rise in grade that would permit them to buy a house in Chevy Chase. It scarcely knew what to make of the invasion of eager professors. A magazine noted, "Professors are the fad," and a reporter observed: "On a routine administration matter you go to a Cabinet member, but on matters of policy and the higher statesmanship you consult the professoriat."

Conservatives were discountenanced by the intellectuals' sudden gain in prestige. That perennial social critic H. L. Mencken sputtered that the academicians were "the sorriest lot of mountebanks ever gathered together at one time, even in Washington . . . professional uplifters and do-gooders . . . poor dubs . . . blatant and intolerable idiots." Mencken was not alone in resenting the university graduates. Yet this new infusion of talent gave to the national government an *élan* sorely missing in the past. Academic friends of Roosevelt, including Harvard's Felix Frankfurter, sent to Washington a corps of brilliant young lawyers—e.g., David Lilienthal and Jerome Frank—who, immensely confident of their ability, generated new ideas, tested new methods and conveyed an infectious enthusiasm for the possibilities of governing.

The President's new Indian commissioner, John Collier, was a former social worker. When he took office he found Indians impoverished, their lands disappearing, their customs repressed. By 1933 Indians had lost two thirds of their land to white men. At the age of six, Indian children were taken from their families to boarding schools which sought to alienate them from their tribal beliefs. Collier closed the boarding schools and got PWA funds to finance Indian schools, weeded out incompetent and dishonest officials, forbade the sale of Indian lands, and ordered reservation and agency officials to respect tribal customs. No one had ever done so much to preserve the unique character of the Indian against the encroachments of white civilization.

I N the process of pushing his program, Roosevelt was rewriting the agenda of American politics. In 1932 men had argued about the tariff, war debts and government economy; in 1936 they were debating valley authorities, public housing and industrial unionism.

To acquaint the nation with these issues, the President undertook a great program of political education. He consciously used his press conferences to instruct newspapermen—and through them the country—about the complicated new problems with which the government was dealing. He was fond of calling the conference place his "schoolroom" and often employed terms like "seminar" or the budget "textbook." When, in January 1934, the President called 35 Washington correspondents to his study, he explained his budget message to them, a magazine reported, "like a football coach going through skull practice with his squad."

At his very first press conference, Roosevelt abolished the written questions that had been required by his predecessor and told reporters they could shoot questions at him without warning (although they were not permitted to use his answers in direct quotations). Columnist Tom Stokes wrote afterward: "The doubters among us—and I was one of them—predicted that the free and open conferences would last a few weeks and then would be aban-

Rexford Guy Tugwell was once chosen by the readers of a Washington paper as the handsomest New Dealer. Conservatives considered him radical but he denied it. "Liberals," Tugwell once wrote, "would like to rebuild the station while the trains are running; radicals prefer to blow up the station."

Raymond Moley began advising F.D.R. in 1928, headed his brain trust and long helped write his speeches. Basically conservative, he parted with Roosevelt soon after Tom Corcoran tried to get Moley to alter an F.D.R. speech in 1936. "You write the music," Corcoran claimed. "He only sings it."

doned." But twice a week, with rare exceptions, year in and year out, the President submitted to the cross fire of questions, some of them rough ones. Reporters had never seen anything like it.

Roosevelt also was the first President to recognize the potentialities of the radio for projecting his ideas and his personality directly into American homes. In his fireside chats he seemed like a father talking about public affairs while sitting with his family in the living room. His voice—a "rich, perfect voice," wrote reporters Joseph Alsop and Turner Catledge, "with the odd trace of an aboriginal Bostonian flatness"—conveyed both authority and warmth. When Roosevelt got before a microphone, grumbled one critic, he appeared to be talking and toasting marshmallows at the same time.

As a New York patrician, Roosevelt came naturally by his paternal attitude toward his constituents. He had a country squire's contempt for the businessman—and a squire's sense of *noblesse oblige* for the less fortunate. Yet the President had, too, a squire's sense of tradition and a conservative regard for property rights. Roosevelt's critics on the right charged repeatedly that he was fostering a socialist conspiracy. But the President had other aims entirely. He hoped to preserve the institution of capitalism by reforming it. Often damned as a traitor to his class, Roosevelt actually averted serious class conflict by his wise concessions.

If the New Deal had been postponed four years, Roosevelt once told newspapermen, it might have come too late. In off-the-record remarks at a press conference in September 1936, he said the situation in America might have been the same as that which had faced Premier Léon Blum when he came to power in France in June of that year.

"Suppose Brother Hoover had remained President until April 1936, carrying on his policies of the previous four years; in other words, hadn't taken any steps towards social security or helping the farmer or cutting out child labor and shortening hours, and old-age pensions. Had that been the case, we would have been a country this past April very similar to the country that Blum found when he came in. The French for 25 or 30 years had never done a thing in the way of social legislation. Blum started in and he jumped right into the middle of a strike the first week he was in office. Well, they demanded a 48-hour week. . . . Then they demanded a one week's holiday with pay and then they demanded, immediately, a commission to set up an old-age pension plan. Well, all of these Blum got through. But, query, was it too late?"

Neither Roosevelt nor his Cabinet officers had any intentions of establishing a socialist state. In the spring of 1933 the President's aides actually were nonplused when harried coal operators came to Washington and invited the government to take over the mines. Frances Perkins recalls that she, the spokesman of the allegedly radical New Deal, found herself reassuring the operators: " 'Now take courage, Mr. X. You can do it. You'll be able to run these mines.' Ickes whispered to me, 'What in the world would we do with the mines if we took them over? Nobody in this Government knows how to run a coal mine.' "

No one protested more loudly that the New Deal was not socialism than the Socialist leader, Norman Thomas. "Mr. Roosevelt," Thomas insisted, "did not carry out the Socialist platform unless he carried it out on a stretcher." Instead of nationalizing the banks, Roosevelt had revived them and turned

The demagogic Governor "Alfalfa Bill" Murray of Oklahoma was one of the most colorful political figures of the 1930s. A Texan who claimed descent from Pocahontas, he ran as a reformer. But once elected he increased the state payroll by 1,000, finding jobs for numerous relatives and friends. His campaign chauffeur became head of a school for the feeble-minded.

them back to private bankers; instead of helping the poor farmer, he had put through the AAA scheme to subsidize scarcity; instead of national planning, he had sponsored the NRA program to stabilize capitalism. Ruefully, Thomas had to concede that Roosevelt's appeal was more successful than his own. In the election of 1936 Thomas polled only 188,000 votes compared to the 882,000 he had received four years before. By 1940 the Socialist vote had sunk to 99,500.

If Roosevelt was not a socialist, neither was he a spokesman for limited government. He believed in a vast extension of the powers of the state even when such an expansion challenged traditional business prerogatives. Business had become accustomed to regard its own interests as paramount and to view government either as its adjutant or as a rival power. Roosevelt rejected this view. He told a national convention of bankers in 1934 that "a true function of the head of the government of the United States is to find among many discordant elements that unity of purpose that is best for the nation as a whole. This is necessary because government is not merely one of many coordinate groups in the community or the nation, but . . . must be the judge of the conflicting interests of all groups in the community, including bankers."

Bank robber John Dillinger, most notorious public enemy of the '30s until the FBI gunned him down, displays the tools of his trade. He delighted in his fame, which he earned by holding up 12 banks in six states in little more than a year. A dashing lawbreaker, he compared himself to Jesse James and told reporters cheerfully he guessed he was "just a born criminal."

ROOSEVELT'S insistence that there was a national interest separate from the business interest and superior to it served to justify an enormous growth in the prestige and power of the federal government. This was certainly the most important single phenomenon of the 1930s.

Nothing better illustrates the loss of faith in local government and the new prestige of the federal government than the nation's changing attitudes toward crime detection. With few exceptions the apprehension and punishment of lawbreakers had always been a local function. But in the '30s local government proved inadequate to deal with the new gangs, which often operated not in a single city but over a wide region. Centered in the Mississippi valley, they had headquarters in St. Paul and Kansas City, with a vast network of hideouts in the Ozarks and in Oklahoma and a small army of informers, fences and even doctors to bind their wounds. They were equipped with submachine guns and high-powered cars, and these often gave them a substantial technological advantage over local police.

The country was so shocked by the brazenness of the criminals and the helplessness of local police that it approved an unprecedented extension of federal authority to deal with particular crimes. It was made a federal crime to assault a federal officer or to rob a federal bank. For the first time agents of the Federal Bureau of Investigation were given blanket authority to carry arms. On March 1, 1932, the son of Charles and Anne Morrow Lindbergh was kidnaped from his crib at Hopewell, New Jersey, and murdered. Congress responded to the national sense of outrage by adopting the "Lindbergh law" which—as toughened by later amendments—made virtually any kidnaping a federal offense, with death as the maximum penalty.

But it took the career of the notorious bandit John Dillinger to create an entirely new pattern of federal authority. After a series of crimes, which culminated when he engineered the escape of 10 convicts from the penitentiary at Michigan City, Indiana, Dillinger was captured and jailed in Lima, Ohio, in September 1933. Within two weeks his confederates had released him and killed the sheriff. In January 1934, after bank robberies in Racine, Wisconsin, and East Chicago, Indiana, Dillinger was apprehended in Tucson, Arizona, and returned to prison in Crown Point, Indiana.

There he was treated as a returning hero; he was photographed with the arm of the prosecuting attorney affectionately draped around him. The woman sheriff of the county, Lillian Holley, boasted that Dillinger was at last locked up in a jail from which he could not escape. In a little more than a month Dillinger had carved a wooden pistol with a razor blade, blackened it with shoe polish, bluffed his way out of prison and driven off in the sheriff's car. While 5,000 officers pursued him, the bank robber made a leisurely stop for a haircut and enjoyed a home cooked Sunday dinner with his family in his hometown. When Dillinger needed arms, he simply raided the Warsaw, Indiana, police station.

Dillinger's exploits, one periodical noted, touched off "a national storm of shame and indignation." But up to that point Dillinger had broken no federal law. When the outlaw left the Indiana jail for Chicago, however, he made a fatal blunder; he crossed a state line in a stolen car, thus violating the 1919 Dyer Act—and permitting the Federal Bureau of Investigation to enter the case. On July 22, 1934, acting on a tip from a Chicago madam, FBI agents shot down John Dillinger as he emerged from a neighborhood movie house (the theme of the movie: Crime does not pay).

The FBI now declared war on bandits. That fall FBI men killed Pretty Boy Floyd near East Liverpool, Ohio; in November they shot Baby Face Nelson, Public Enemy No. 1, near Barrington, Illinois; in May 1936 the chief of the bureau, J. Edgar Hoover, personally arrested Alvin Karpis, wanted for murder and kidnaping, outside Karpis' apartment on Canal Street in New Orleans. Sometimes FBI men blundered, sometimes the bureau received credit which belonged to local police or to Treasury agents. But the published exploits of the FBI helped persuade many Americans that only the federal government could deal adequately with serious national problems.

IN the 1936 presidential campaign Roosevelt faced his first direct political challenge since he had assumed office in March 1933. Herbert Hoover was still in such disfavor that the Republicans did not dare nominate him again in 1936; instead they named Governor Alf Landon of Kansas, the only G.O.P. chief executive who had won election in both 1932 and 1934. His running mate was Colonel Frank Knox, a Chicago newspaper publisher who had been a Rough Rider under Theodore Roosevelt at San Juan Hill.

Republican leaders presented Landon as living proof that humanitarianism did not require unbalanced budgets and wild fiscal theories. "There are people today calling themselves liberals," said Landon, "who regard any suggestion of economy as reactionary." Although Landon's reputation as a budget balancer rested in good part on the money the New Deal had poured into Kansas, his claim that he was a progressive was well founded. He had been a Bull Moose county chairman in 1912; he had backed William Allen White in his campaign against the Ku Klux Klan in the 1920s; as governor he had strengthened regulation of business and had refused to sanction a proposed investigation of alleged "Red" activities in the state university.

Landon's greatest handicap was that the Hoover wing of the party took the campaign away from him, and most of the country never became aware that

Bullets fly in the Louisiana State House as bodyguards riddle Dr. Carl Weiss, the slayer of Senator Huey Long, 42 (foreground). The swaggering Kingfish lived in fear for his life and was always surrounded by guards; one of them was almost shot down in the fusillade that followed the assassination. Afterward, 61 bullet holes were counted in the killer's body.

Caricatured as the Three Musketeers, Gerald L. K. Smith, Dr. Francis Townsend and Father Charles Coughlin are shown (from left to right) wrangling over who will lead their right-wing alliance. The priest won the contest but incurred the displeasure of Church officials —including a virtually unprecedented public reproof from the Vatican—for calling Roosevelt a liar.

the governor had a modestly liberal record. Landon's running mate and the party chairman, John Hamilton, made extravagant charges that President Roosevelt was directing a sinister conspiracy. "The New Deal candidate," Knox insisted, "has been leading us toward Moscow."

Against a candidate as dynamic as Franklin Roosevelt, Landon was badly mismatched. Most Americans thought of the Kansan as a colorless man; he spoke poorly, especially when contrasted with the eloquent Roosevelt. "He turned out, indeed," mourned H. L. Mencken, "to be one of the worst public speakers recorded in the archives of faunal zoology." Moreover, Landon seemed to many to be no more than a fair-to-middling prairie-state governor who lacked Roosevelt's preparation for dealing with the problems of the nation and the world.

For many months the Republicans had been wooing conservative Democrats who disapproved of Roosevelt's New Deal. As early as the fall of 1933 Alfred E. Smith, who had been the Democratic presidential candidate in 1928, had attacked the national Administration. In January 1936, speaking at a banquet in Washington, Smith angrily accused the New Dealers of pursuing a socialist course. "It is all right with me if they want to disguise themselves as Karl Marx or Lenin or any of the rest of that bunch," he shouted, "but I won't stand for their allowing them to march under the banner of Jackson or Cleveland."

Smith had made his speech at a banquet sponsored by the American Liberty League, an organization founded in 1934 by a group of Northern industrialists and disaffected Democrats, including John J. Raskob, a Du Pont executive who had once been national Democratic chairman. The Liberty League claimed to be an alliance of liberty-loving Americans of all classes, but it was obviously backed by the rich. It was never able to form a labor or farm division. Every time the League issued a statement, Roosevelt won more votes. By the summer of 1936 it had become so unpopular that the Republicans asked it to stop giving public support to Landon.

IN all respects Roosevelt was fortunate in his enemies. Many of those who protested they were suffering harshly under the New Deal actually led lives of opulence, yet they kept accusing relievers—who could barely survive on the few dollars they were granted each month—of "living in luxury." Robert Wood, president of Sears, Roebuck, said: "While it is probably true that we cannot allow everyone to starve (although I personally disagree with this philosophy and the philosophy of the city social worker) . . . if relief is to be given it must be on a bare subsistence allowance." The Rev. George B. Cutten, president of Colgate University, warned that social legislation endangered the race and that the "unfit" should be permitted to die off.

It was apparent that Republican hopes rested less on such support as this than on the possibility that a combination of dissidents under the leadership of Huey Long would attract a number of votes from Roosevelt, thus allowing the G.O.P. challenger to slip through. By 1935 Long's ambitions were boundless; so, many believed, were his prospects. But that September Dr. Carl Austin Weiss, who had been incensed by Long's attempt to oust Weiss's father-in-law from a judgeship, stepped out of the shadows at the Louisiana state house and shot Long to death.

The assassination removed Roosevelt's most dangerous rival. Gerald L. K.

Smith, the leader of Long's Share-Our-Wealth organization, looked for another national leader to whom he could attach himself. Of all the Pied Pipers in view, Dr. Francis Townsend seemed the likeliest possibility. In the West, Townsendism was a political force which bedeviled leaders of both parties. A poll of editors taken by the Portland *Oregonian* indicated that the Townsendites had the power to decide the outcome of most congressional races in Washington, California, Oregon, Idaho, Nevada and Colorado. In June 1936 the Smith-Townsend forces joined with Father Coughlin to create a new third party. The presidential candidate of the Union party was Representative William Lemke of North Dakota.

The Union party campaign had hardly gotten under way when it began to fall apart. Coughlin quickly shouldered the other leaders aside and seized control. Gerald Smith could not win Long's followers to himself; Townsend and Lemke both denounced Smith for his fascist sympathies. Coughlin's violent tirades—he said the choice between Roosevelt and Landon was one between carbolic acid and rat poison—not only disquieted former admirers but led his own church to chastise him.

THE disintegration of the Union party campaign enhanced the prospects of Franklin Roosevelt. By 1936 Roosevelt had forged a new political coalition based on the masses in the great Northern cities. This political combination won the allegiance of a diverse group of leaders: machine bosses such as Jersey City's Frank Hague, progressive Republicans including New York City's Mayor Fiorello La Guardia and, most important, a new kind of urban Democrat typified by Pittsburgh's Mayor David Lawrence who not only supported Roosevelt's national social reforms but inaugurated "little New Deals" in their own states.

Under Governor George Earle, Pennsylvania's Little New Deal levied heavy taxes on corporations, set maximum hours for women and children, abolished imprisonment for failure to pay local taxes and permitted the creation of rural electric co-operatives. It eliminated the detested coal and iron police and forbade corporations to hire deputy sheriffs. The Pennsylvania legislature passed a new workmen's compensation law with benefits so sweeping that the United Mine Workers protested that the measure might injure the coal industry.

Emblems of defeat, these 1936 campaign buttons touted the presidential hopes of Alf Landon (above) and William Lemke (below). The sunflower was the symbol of Landon's home state of Kansas, and Republicans flooded the country with sunflower buttons and posters in 1936. Democrats responded with automobile stickers that noted: "Sunflowers die in November."

New York, under Governor Herbert Lehman, extended workmen's compensation, provided for unemployment insurance, raised the minimum age for children leaving school to enter industry and outlawed "yellow-dog" contracts, under which workers had to promise their employers that they would not join a union. Labor leader George Meany called it the greatest social program ever passed by any American state.

The New Deal coalition was based on a series of special appeals to separate groups. Notable among these were the Negroes. As late as 1932 American Negroes were still solidly Republican. Chicago's heavily Negro Ward 3 gave Roosevelt only 20.7 per cent of the vote that year. But in 1934, in response to the benefits of the New Deal, Negroes began to switch to the Democrats. In many areas Negroes were surviving largely because of relief checks. Of the two million people the WPA taught to read, more than 400,000 were Negroes. Roosevelt gave Negroes prominent seats at his inauguration and appointed Negroes to more important posts than they had ever held in a Democratic administration. Between 1933 and 1940 he named 133 people of this race to federal positions. In 1936 more than half of Chicago's Ward 3 voted Democratic.

Negroes were especially impressed by the work of Mrs. Roosevelt. She not only pleaded for racial tolerance but worked actively with leaders of the National Association for the Advancement of Colored People to influence the President.

Another group of voters cultivated by the New Deal were the nation's women. The President had set the pattern at the beginning of his Administration by naming the first woman ever appointed to a Cabinet post, Secretary of Labor Perkins. Mrs. Roosevelt dramatized the woman's vote in public affairs. She became the most politically active First Lady in history. She traveled widely, spoke out on a variety of subjects and poked about in places where injustice had too long been permitted to fester.

But perhaps the most important element in Roosevelt's coalition was union labor. In the 1936 campaign John L. Lewis, a lifelong Republican, mobilized his battalions behind the President, stating: "Labor has gained more under President Roosevelt than any President in memory." In 1932 labor unions had made almost no contribution to the Roosevelt cause. In 1936, by contrast, the Democrats got $770,000 from unions, nearly $500,000 of this from the United Mine Workers. (In the preceding 30 years the total contributed to national political campaigns by the AFL had been $95,000.)

In addition to union members, a surprising number of businessmen voted for Roosevelt. In particular, Roosevelt had the warm support of leaders in such newer industries as motion pictures and radio. The Boston merchant Edward Filene declared that although the government took half his income each year in taxes, "when I see what my country is getting for its money now, I consider this taxpaying the best bargain of my life."

Roosevelt was grateful for such support, but he was acutely aware that most of big business bitterly opposed him. In his annual message to Congress in January 1936, he attacked men who sought to "gang up against the people's liberties" and spoke of having "earned the hatred of entrenched greed." As he entered the campaign he seemed, at times, to take a puckish delight in the opposition of the rich and well-born. At Harvard's tercentenary celebration in 1936, Roosevelt pointed out that at the 200th anniversary celebration a century before "many of the alumni of Harvard were sorely troubled by the state of the nation. Andrew Jackson was President. On the 250th anniversary of the founding of Harvard College, alumni again were sorely troubled. Grover Cleveland was President." He paused. "Now, on the 300th anniversary, I am President."

Postmaster General James A. Farley was renowned for his spectacular memory. It was said that he never forgot a face or a name, and Farley himself declared he could call up a friend in every city from Maine to California. "Someone once asked me if I thought I had 50,000 friends," he said. "Without wanting to brag, I think 100,-000 comes closer to the number."

IN the last days of the campaign the Republicans warned workers they might never see their social security deductions again; John Hamilton, the G.O.P. national chairman, even said that every employee would have to wear a metal dog tag for life. Angered, Roosevelt made an unrestrained attack on his opponents. At Madison Square Garden on the eve of the election he charged: "For twelve years this nation was afflicted with hear-nothing, see-nothing, do-nothing government." Business leaders, he said, "had begun to consider the government of the United States as a mere appendage to their own affairs. We know now that government by organized money is just as dangerous as government by organized mob. Never before in all our history have these forces been so united against one candidate as they stand today. They are unanimous in their hate for me—and I welcome their hatred."

Roosevelt campaigned as the leader of a liberal crusade which cut across party lines. Some of the chief campaigners, men like Harold Ickes and Henry Wallace, were old-time Republicans. In Nebraska Roosevelt snubbed the Democratic nominee and endorsed independent Senator George Norris; in Wisconsin the New Dealers worked with La Follette Progressives; in Minnesota the Democrats withdrew their ticket in favor of the Farmer-Labor slate.

Roosevelt had come a long way in four years, and he was sometimes embarrassed by the need to square his actions in his first term with his campaign pledges of 1932. As the President made plans to speak in Pittsburgh in 1936, he asked his adviser and speechwriter, Judge Samuel Rosenman, to work out an address that would demonstrate that his policies had been consistent with his 1932 speech in that city, when he had urged a slash in government spending. That evening Rosenman said he thought he had found a way to resolve the dilemma of the 1932 speech: "Deny categorically that you ever made it." In his 1936 Pittsburgh speech, Roosevelt justified the switch in policies this way: "To balance our budget in 1933 or 1934 or 1935 would have been a crime against the American people. When Americans suffered we refused to pass by on the other side. Humanity came first."

Mayor Frank Hague, Democratic boss of Jersey City who once told a constituent "I am the law," is depicted as the angel Gabriel summoning deceased voters to the polls. A voter who registered once remained on the rolls, and—as a contemporary put it—"somehow the registered dead of Hudson County continue to be politically active for years after their demise."

THE economic upsurge of 1936 appeared to justify the Administration's program. Roosevelt's main campaign theme was the contrast between America in 1936 and the America of 1932. From 1931 through 1933, there had been 6,000 bank failures (including, presumably, a few following the 1933 bank holiday); from 1934 through 1936 there had been 166. The stock market in 1936 was climbing steadily. Industrial output was 65 per cent higher than at the low point of the Depression. So much new construction was started that Pacific Northwest sawmills could not keep pace with lumber orders.

To be sure, there were weak spots. In the seventh year of the Depression eight million Americans still had no jobs. Industrial production had still not reached 1929 figures, and corporate profits were only a little more than half those of 1929. But there was an unmistakable smell of prosperity in the air.

As Roosevelt toured the country, the enthusiastic response of crowds staggered veterans of previous campaigns. In January Roosevelt guessed the Republicans would capture 216 electoral votes; in early August he still gave them 191. The President's campaign manager, Postmaster General James Farley, was more optimistic. On November 2 Farley wrote the President: "I am still definitely of the opinion that you will carry every state but two—Maine and Vermont."

The election results bore out Farley's prediction precisely. With 523 votes to Landon's 8, Roosevelt was re-elected by the most sweeping electoral margin of any candidate since James Monroe. His popular vote was 27,753,000; Landon's, 16,675,000; Lemke's, 882,000. Never had a major political party sustained as devastating a defeat as the Republicans in 1936. "As Maine goes," Farley jeered, "so goes Vermont." The Republican editor William Allen White commented: "It was not an election the country has just undergone, but a political Johnstown flood." His policies vindicated, his opponents all but annihilated, Franklin Roosevelt was at the crest of his fortunes.

THE HAPPY PAST is evoked by the cast of the Broadway hit *Life with Father* in this caricature by Al Hirschfeld. Father, seen eyeing the children, was played by Howard Lindsay, a coauthor of the play. Mother *(left)* was portrayed by Dorothy Stickney.

Pleasures to brighten a drab time

URING the depression-ridden '30s Americans sought entertainment that helped them forget their troubles. They went to the movies, where they could see a double feature for as little as a dime. The screenplays that Hollywood concocted for the new generation of stars were usually lighthearted and unchallenging. With notable exceptions, such as the *March of Time* documentaries, movies avoided real discontents and disturbing conflicts; their stock in trade was romanticized love, stylish glamor and innocent sex appeal, uncomplicated comedy and adventure. By the mid-'30s, some 60 per cent of all Americans were attending movies every week.

Even more people listened regularly to the radio, which brought a carefree world into the home itself. The variety show—a good-natured potpourri of songs, jokes, comedy skits and commercials—became the standard format for a dozen enormously popular entertainers. The nation, bound together by quick radio coverage of the news, listened with avid interest to developments in the Lindbergh kidnaping case and the subsequent trial of Bruno Hauptmann; and millions gasped in horror at an eyewitness description of the burning of the dirigible *Hindenburg* at Lakehurst, New Jersey. Radio made its own news: In 1938, when the young actor Orson Welles dramatized a science-fiction invasion from outer space, thousands panicked all over the country. The medium also helped popularize the big swing bands, whose teen-age enthusiasts were viewed with alarm by almost every adult.

In the '30s play productions, like book sales, declined sharply. Although the theater did not hesitate to present dramas of social realism, some of its best-known plays were musicals and comedies. *Life with Father (above)*, which ran for a record 3,224 performances, was in the mainstream of escape entertainment. Like Hollywood's output, it offered audiences an unattainable world —in this case a bygone time whose simple contentment had vanished forever.

BEHAVING SCANDALOUSLY in the Civil War epic *Gone With the Wind*, Scarlett O'Hara (Vivien Leigh) attends a ball in Atlanta while dressed in mourning for her husband. Even worse, she is obviously enjoying her dance with the raffish blockade-runner Rhett Butler (Clark Gable). The film, costliest production of the '30s, became Hollywood's biggest money-maker.

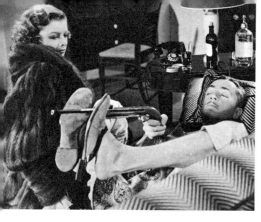

OFFBEAT COMEDY, *The Thin Man* presented William Powell as a madcap detective, Myrna Loy as his wife.

WESTERN ADVENTURE, staple film fare in the '30s, reached a high point in *Stagecoach*, with Claire Trevor and John Wayne.

GLAMOROUS STARS Greta Garbo and John Barrymore headed a cast of many movie greats in the lavish *Grand Hotel*.

SONG AND DANCE were presented stylishly by Fred Astaire and Ginger Rogers, shown here in *Carefree*.

INJUSTICE was a major theme of *The Life of Emile Zola*, a serious film for its day, starring the celebrated actor Paul Muni.

OPERETTA brought together the singers Nelson Eddy and Jeanette MacDonald in eight films. This one was *Sweethearts*.

HORROR MOVIES were sure-fire hits. The *Bride of Frankenstein* featured Elsa Lanchester and Boris Karloff.

FARCE AND SLAPSTICK, specialties of the frantic Marx Brothers, were displayed in this scene from *A Day at the Races*.

SENTIMENTALITY was unrestrained in *Little Miss Marker*, Shirley Temple's first important role, with Adolphe Menjou.

Familiar faces in the film world of make-believe

IN the '30s, writes historian Arthur M. Schlesinger Jr., "films mattered in American life. . . . Young men sauntered down the street like James Cagney, wise-cracked like William Powell, cursed like Humphrey Bogart and wooed like Clark Gable; young women laughed like Lombard and sighed like Garbo and looked (or tried to look) like Hedy Lamarr." These were but a few of the deities of the Hollywood pantheon. Millions of Americans followed their idols' screen careers with avid interest, and between visits to more than 15,000 movie houses they gobbled up the gossip about the stars' private lives, which was reported in newspapers and fan magazines. The movies themselves, which leaned toward sentiment, farce and fantasy, were often panned by serious critics. But the fan in the darkened theater found the reassurance he wanted. In the comfortable half-world of film, women were beautiful, men were handsome and success always lurked around the corner.

FIRST FULL-LENGTH ANIMATED FILM, Walt Disney's 1937 *Snow White and the Seven Dwarfs,* was called "the happiest thing . . . since the armistice." It utilized 250,000 drawings.

IN "THE WIZARD OF OZ," Judy Garland dries the tears of the Cowardly Lion (Bert Lahr). Their companions are the Tin Woodman (Jack Haley), at left, and the Scarecrow (Ray Bolger).

Fred Allen (right) threatens Jack Benny while Portland Hoffa (left) and Mary Livingstone add to the confusion in an obviously contrived

IMPRESARIO OF TALENT, Major Edward Bowes hits his gong, signaling the failure of an amateur to win his approval. Many of Bowes's "amateurs" were actually unemployed professionals.

On the air, entertainment for every mood and taste

FOR millions of Americans in the '30s, the radio was a daily ritual. The "monster," as critics of radio called the home set, came in all sizes and shapes. Out of all the speakers, thanks to nationwide network broadcasting, came the same programs. Radio performers developed a following as loyal as that of the movie stars; every week the fans tuned in for the droll insults of Edgar Bergen and Charlie McCarthy, the songs of Bing Crosby and Kate Smith *(right)*, the sometimes painful offerings of Major Bowes's amateurs. Soap operas like "Ma Perkins" and "Just Plain Bill" kept housewives company.

Yet despite the banality of most programs, radio also brought fine music, sports and public affairs to countless shut-ins. Boake Carter reported the news, H. V. Kaltenborn analyzed it and Gabriel Heatter made melodramatic comments on it. ("There is no smile on Hitler's face tonight.")

But laughter was what America wanted, and on March 14, 1937, when sardonic Fred Allen met waspish Jack Benny *(above)*, their audience was exceeded only by those attracted by President Roosevelt's fireside chats.

"feud" which many listeners took seriously.

MASTER OF CEREMONIES Rudy Vallee, a popular bandleader and crooner, shows violinist Dave Rubinoff how to conduct.

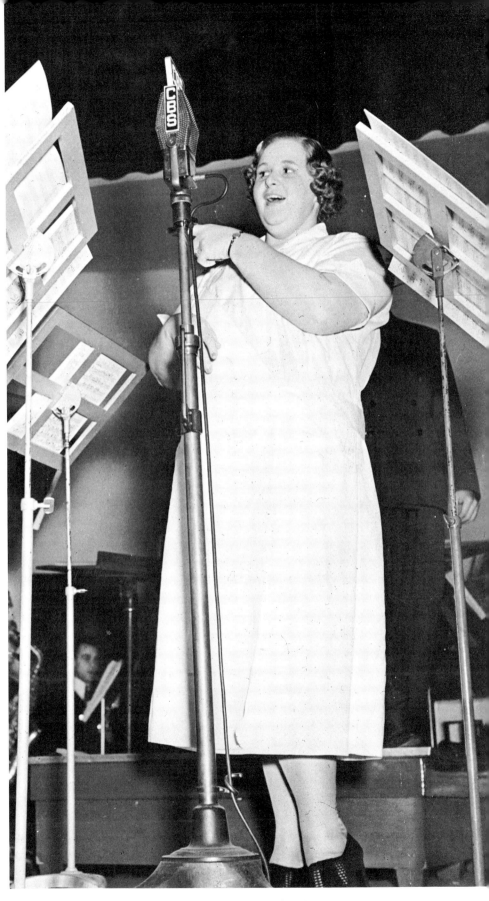

"THE SONGBIRD OF THE SOUTH," Kate Smith opens a broadcast with her cheery "Hello, everybody." F.D.R., in introducing her to the visiting King of England, said, "This is America."

THE BIG APPLE, essentially a swing version of the square dance, is performed by "jitterbugs" at the Glen Island Casino, New Rochelle, New York, a popular rendezvous for swing fans.

Getting in the groove with swing's athletic apostles

WHILE most Americans danced leisurely to the music of Paul Whiteman and Guy Lombardo, swing bands attracted a young, noisy, athletic following. Devotees of swing, a lively music based on the jazz of New Orleans, gyrated wildly (above), shouting encouragement to their heroes—Benny Goodman (right), Tommy Dorsey, Artie Shaw, Glenn Miller. The fans spoke a language full of odd expressions like "in the groove."

The swing fever may have reached its height in 1938, when 23,000 youngsters crowded into a "Carnival of Swing" at Randall's Island in New York. Fully 25 bands took turns playing through 5 hours 45 minutes of sheer pandemonium. The police were hard put to protect the musicians from what the New York *Times* called "destruction by admiration," a form of frenzied mayhem hitherto unknown to most upholders of law and order.

THE KING OF SWING, Benny Goodman, leads his band in a "Battle of Swing" at Harlem's Savoy Ballroom. Goodman is often credited with having started the swing craze.

4. THE END
OF THE
NEW DEAL

AFTER Franklin Roosevelt's smashing triumph in the 1936 elections, a writer for the New York *Times* observed: "If he were to say a kind word for the man-eating shark, people would look thoughtful and say perhaps there *are* two sides to the question." So powerful did the President's victory coalition seem that people seriously pondered whether the Republican party, like the Federalist party of 1800, was not finished as a national force. Yet within one year the President was a badly beaten political leader whose coalition was disintegrating and whose hopes for yet another era of long-needed reforms had all but vanished.

The New Deal came to an end because the forces of resistance to change saw the opportunity in 1937 to offer more effective opposition to the "Roosevelt Revolution." They gained this opportunity when three separate events—Roosevelt's attempt to "pack" the Supreme Court, the wave of sit-down strikes and the recession of 1937-1938—weakened the President's hold on a large segment of his followers.

The nation's middle class had become growingly uneasy about the consequences of the New Deal. Members of this group admired much of what Roosevelt had done: the rescue of the banks, the economic revival, the various welfare measures. But they were dismayed by two particular developments: the growth in power of the federal government and the enhanced authority of lower-income groups, especially of the labor unions, which challenged

GOVERNMENT ACTIVITIES under F.D.R. are represented by a TVA worker *(left)*, a lawyer *(center)* pleading the gold case before the high court, and a Land Office surveyor.

Justice Louis Brandeis practiced severe austerity. He ate simple fare from a table without a cloth, got to his office at 6 a.m. carrying a lunch of two sandwiches and often wrote his own letters in longhand. "I have only one life," he said, "and it's short enough. Why waste it on things I don't want?"

Although Justice Harlan Stone was a Republican—he was Attorney General under Coolidge and played medicine ball with Hoover —he criticized Court colleagues for striking down the Democrats' laws. "Courts," he said, "are concerned only with the power to enact statutes, not with their wisdom."

their own prerogatives. The events of 1937 greatly reinforced these anxieties.

The President's troubles began only two weeks after his second inauguration, when he stunned the nation by asking for the addition of a number of new justices to the U.S. Supreme Court. The request set off a chain reaction which ultimately splintered the Democratic party, jeopardized Roosevelt's popularity and shortened the life of the New Deal. Later the President's critics would charge him with a monumental blunder. Yet however maladroit the Roosevelt move may have been in form and execution, some attempt to reform the Court could hardly have been postponed. The Court's own actions in the past three years had invited a head-on clash with the President.

FROM the very beginning, the New Dealers had feared that the Court would invalidate reform legislation. Four of the justices—James McReynolds, George Sutherland, Willis Van Devanter and Pierce Butler—were staunch conservatives. Three judges—Louis Brandeis, Benjamin Cardozo and Harlan Fiske Stone—seemed safely in the New Deal camp. But if either of the two men in the center—Chief Justice Charles Evans Hughes or Owen Roberts— joined the conservative four, the conservatives would prevail.

The architects of the New Deal hoped that the Court would recognize the Depression to be an extraordinary emergency which justified exceptional extensions of governmental power. For a time it appeared that the Court might be taking just such a view. In a series of 5-4 decisions in 1934 and early 1935, it supported stronger governmental authority in cases involving a mortgage moratorium law, the setting of minimum and maximum retail prices for milk and the federal repudiation of the gold clause in government bonds. But in this last instance the Court questioned the constitutionality of the government's action. Many believed that the majority had been coerced into validating the repudiation of gold out of fear that any other decision would have meant financial chaos. Some observers predicted that the Court would seize the first opportunity to right the scales.

On May 27, 1935, the ax fell. In a unanimous decision the Court demolished a cornerstone of Roosevelt's program, the National Industrial Recovery Act, on the ground that the Administration's attempt to regulate the business of the Schechter brothers, who ran a poultry jobbing firm in Brooklyn, represented an unconstitutional delegation of executive power and an illegal attempt to exercise authority over intrastate commerce. This disrupted the government's campaign for economic mobilization and it gave the President's enemies their first real opportunity to rejoice since he took office. The Hearst newspapers delightedly removed the Blue Eagle from their mastheads and ran American flags instead.

Early in 1936 the Court struck at another cornerstone of the New Deal by ruling the processing tax of the Agricultural Adjustment Act unconstitutional. Few decisions aroused more indignation. In a biting dissent Justice Stone declared that "language, even of a constitution, may mean what it says." The decision appeared to block any attempt of the government to deal with the difficult problem of the agricultural depression.

On June 1, 1936, the Court declared the New York minimum wage law unconstitutional, holding that the state was "without power by any form of legislation to prohibit, change or nullify contracts between employers and adult women workers as to the amount of wages to be paid." Harold Ickes noted angrily in his diary: "The sacred right of liberty of contract again—the right of an immature child or a helpless woman to drive a bargain with a great corporation."

Men of the most varied political views were appalled by the Court's wage ruling. It appeared to deny any government, state or federal, any kind of authority over working conditions. Herbert Hoover proposed a constitutional amendment to give back to the states "the power they thought they already had." At the end of the session, Associate Justice Stone wrote: "We finished the term of Court yesterday, I think in many ways one of the most disastrous in its history."

Well before the end of 1936, Roosevelt was giving serious thought to finding some way to make the Court more responsive to the needs of the times. Not only had the Court invalidated much of the New Deal, but its line of reasoning suggested that it would soon find such statutes as the Wagner National Labor Relations Act and the Social Security Act unconstitutional too. To be sure, Roosevelt might simply wait until one or more justices resigned or died, but no one could foresee how long a period this would be. Not a single justice had left the bench in his entire first term, and his legislative program faced paralysis.

Yet none of the proposals suggested—a constitutional amendment to limit the Court's authority was the most popular idea—seemed likely to meet the problem posed by the Court's intransigence. Roosevelt was convinced that a constitutional amendment would not be ratified by enough states, at least not in a reasonable period of time. "If you were not as scrupulous and ethical as you happen to be," he wrote a prominent New York attorney who favored the amendment process, "you could make five million dollars as easy as rolling off a log by undertaking a campaign to prevent the ratification by one house of the Legislature, or even the summoning of a constitutional convention in 13 states for the next four years. Easy money." Noting how simple it would be to block an amendment, Ickes said in his diary: "The President told me the other day that Senator Neely, of West Virginia, had said that $25,000 would do the trick in his state."

Moreover, any legislation passed under the authorization of such an amendment would still be subject to review by possibly hostile courts. Assistant Attorney General Robert Jackson put it bluntly: "Judges who resort to a tortured construction of the Constitution may torture an amendment. You cannot amend a state of mind."

I N February 1937 Roosevelt unveiled his scheme in a special message to Congress. The President claimed that shortages of personnel had resulted in overcrowded federal court dockets and had occasioned great delay and expense to litigants. "A part of the problem of obtaining a sufficient number of judges to dispose of cases is the capacity of the judges themselves," the President continued. "This brings forward the question of aged or infirm judges—a subject of delicacy and yet one which requires frank discussion."

Life tenure for judges, the President declared, "was not intended to create a static judiciary. A constant and systematic addition of younger blood will vitalize the courts and better equip them to recognize and apply the essential concepts of justice in the light of the needs and the facts of an ever changing world." To help achieve these ends, the President recommended that when a

Cartoons show (above) the birth of NRA, clothed in feathers from the American eagle, and (below) its death, nailed to the wall by the Court. Actually it was already dying. Industry ruled the codes, labor called it "National Run Around," and Hugh Johnson had left, as he put it, in a "hail of dead cats."

federal judge who had served at least 10 years waited more than six months after his 70th birthday to resign or retire, the President might add a new judge to the bench. He could appoint up to six new justices to the Supreme Court and 44 new judges to the lower federal tribunals.

The first congressional response to Roosevelt's message was largely favorable. If the proposal had been pushed to a quick vote, the measure might conceivably have been approved. But Senator Henry Fountain Ashurst, chairman of the Judiciary Committee, kept the hearings going. The Administration made the mistake of presenting its case too briefly, and most of the hearings served to publicize the views of the bill's opponents.

As the hearings continued, opposition to the Court plan mounted. Some men were offended by Roosevelt's deviousness in clothing a stratagem to pack the Court in the dress of an attempt to speed procedures. The proposal, said Hugh Johnson, was "too damned slick." Others objected that the President was tampering with the institutions established by the founding fathers. Although the number of justices on the Court had been changed at least five times before, many Americans believed that the Constitution specified nine members. Among those who objected to the Roosevelt plan were a number of Democratic senators. Senator Carter Glass of Virginia called it "frightful," "shocking," "brutal" and "iniquitous." The opposition of a conservative Democrat like Glass might have been anticipated. More serious for the future of the party was the defection of erstwhile New Deal senators like Burton Wheeler of Montana and Joseph O'Mahoney of Wyoming. At the urging of the shrewd Minority Leader, Charles McNary of Oregon, the Republican senators agreed to keep silent and encourage the Democrats to fight one another on the bill.

The heaviest blow against the Court-packing plan was struck by the Court itself. On May 24 it upheld the Social Security Act. On May 29, in a 5-4 reversal of its previous stand, it upheld a Washington minimum wage statute similar to the New York law it had wiped out. Justice Roberts had switched. Two weeks later Roberts joined in a series of 5-4 decisions which found the Wagner Act constitutional.

These decisions marked a historic change in the doctrines of the Court, but they also erased the most important justification for Roosevelt's Court bill. As one wag said: "A switch in time saved nine." The final blows were struck by a devastating letter by Chief Justice Hughes, demonstrating that Roosevelt's charge of inefficiency was groundless, and the announcement by Justice Van Devanter that he planned to retire from the bench.

In July 1937 the Court bill was sent back to committee. That same month the President named to the vacancy Senator Hugo Black of Alabama, a foe of Southern conservatives. This appointment resulted in a furor a month after Black had been confirmed when evidence came that he had been a member of the Ku Klux Klan. On October 1, 1937, Black spoke to an immense radio audience and announced that he had long since resigned from the Klan and was totally out of sympathy with bigotry. Black survived the episode and in later years more than vindicated his claim that he was neither a racist nor a bigot but a champion of minority rights.

Black was only the first of a series of liberal justices Roosevelt was able to name to the bench. Within 30 months after the rejection of his Court pro-

A cartoon by J. N. "Ding" Darling records the widespread opposition to F.D.R.'s Court bill. Many Democrats deserted him on this issue, fearing a precedent of tampering with the judiciary would be set. "Boys," said the chairman of the House Judiciary Committee, "here's where I cash in." In the Senate, Vice President Garner expressed his opinion of the measure by silently holding his nose.

posal, the President had appointed five of the nine justices: Black, Stanley Reed, Felix Frankfurter, William O. Douglas and Frank Murphy. The new Court—the Roosevelt Court, it was called—progressively weakened the 14th Amendment as a shield for corporations and strengthened it as a protection for minorities. It sustained New Deal statutes and extended widely the authority of the national government to regulate the economy.

Roosevelt might well claim, as he did, that he had lost the battle but won the war. Yet in another sense the President had also lost the war. The Court fight destroyed the unity of the Democratic party and strengthened the President's opponents immeasurably. The new Court might be willing to uphold new laws, but a mutinous Congress would pass few of Roosevelt's measures for the justices to consider.

Many conservative and middle-of-the-road Democrats had believed for some time that the New Deal had gone too far, and the Court issue served as a convenient way to break with the Administration. They could go to the people as the guardians of the Constitution rather than as the opponents of reform. Yet what they really feared was that the Administration had become identified with revolutionary changes in class relations.

Nothing served more to strengthen these fears than the wave of strikes which swept America at the very time that Congress was embroiled in the bitter fight over court packing. In 1936 the union movement had stepped up its tempo. Certain industries had imposed company unions upon their employees; they refused to recognize labor-organized unions or to consider collective bargaining as a legitimate and necessary part of labor-management relations. Sensing that the time was ripe for a major offensive, John L. Lewis boldly rented offices for the Steel Workers Organizing Committee in the Grant Building in Pittsburgh, the very home of several of the country's powerful steel companies. Labor had never been able to organize the steel industry, but if the CIO could crack Big Steel—that is, U.S. Steel, largest of the companies by far—the rest of industry might topple like a tower of dominoes. In the Allegheny Valley organizers quietly made the rounds house-to-house; unionists on assembly lines spread the gospel to fellow workers; secret meetings were held in the woods.

Justice Hugo Black, shown with Vice President Garner (left), was once described in the New York "Times" as the most zealous advocate of human liberty in the Court's history. He was an equally impressive figure on another court: As a tennis player he was famed for a smashing, never-say-die game. One day when he was 75 he played for 3 hours in 90° heat.

B UT the big test was not to come in steel. In late 1935 and early 1936 rubber workers in Akron had made sporadic use of a technique first widely employed in European labor disputes: Instead of walking off the job they sat down at their machines and refused to work. On December 30, 1936, employees seeking recognition for the United Automobile Workers at Fisher Body Plant No. 1 in Flint, Michigan, adopted this "sit-down" method on a large scale. They occupied the entire factory and refused to leave. Sit-down strikes spread through the General Motors empire. For six weeks men lived in the plants, and police attempting to dislodge them were routed in "The Battle of Bulls' Run" by a fusillade of nuts and bolts, steel hinges and coffee mugs. On February 11, 1937, GM capitulated, although it was a few months before the country recognized the full extent of the union triumph.

The UAW followed up its victory at GM with quick triumphs at Chrysler and Packard. The quasi-revolutionary movement toward industrial unionism catapulted new personalities into power almost overnight. At the beginning of the Kelsey-Hayes Wheel strike, young Walter Reuther had 78 members in his local. Ten days later he had 30,000 (by his count) and had won recognition as a powerful figure in Detroit. He later recalled: "A guy we never heard of would call up and say, 'We shut down such-and-such a plant. Send us over some coffee and doughnuts.'"

Less than a month after the General Motors victory came the startling news that U.S. Steel had surrendered to the CIO without a fight. The contract recognized the Steel Workers Organizing Committee as bargaining agent for its members and granted a wage boost and a 40-hour week. By early June 1937 the SWOC, then a year old, claimed 375,000 members; by the end of the month it had brought 142 firms into line, including all the subsidiaries of U.S. Steel and such important independents as Jones & Laughlin. But when the SWOC tried to organize "Little Steel"—Republic, Bethlehem and some other major independents—it ran into a stone wall. These companies decided to fight the SWOC, and the steel workers struck. Despite considerable violence and long, arduous negotiations, Little Steel was able to resist organization until 1942.

NEVERTHELESS, the organizing drive of 1937 radically altered American labor relations. In 1936 the United Electrical and Radio Workers, under 24-year-old James Carey, had carried out a series of futile negotiations with the Radio Corporation of America. By early 1938 not only RCA but General Electric had come to terms with UE; Philco had signed earlier.

Many of the gains were won by the tactic of the sit-down strike. The Electrical Workers even produced a film to teach sit-down techniques. With scenes from the Exide Battery sit-down in Philadelphia, it showed strikers preparing food, giving musical entertainment, sweeping up the plant, barbering one another and doing daily exercises. By early 1937 the sit-down strike had reached epidemic proportions. Wives sat down against penny-pinching husbands; school children sat down against strict teachers; motorists sat down against couldn't-care-less street-repair departments.

A few congressmen rejoiced that this novel stratagem had won for industrial workers gains that would have been possible in no other way. But many lawmakers were outraged by these assaults on property rights and by the refusal of President Roosevelt to use force to dislodge the strikers. Resentment at the Administration's toleration of the sit-down strikes, coupled with anger at the President's attack on the Court, jeopardized the middle-class base of the Roosevelt coalition.

In August 1937 enthusiasm for Roosevelt among members of this group was dealt an even more savage blow. Just when the country appeared to be well on its way out of the Depression, there was a sudden economic setback. The recession of 1937-1938 did not begin to have the consequences of the crash of 1929, but the decline from September 1937 to June 1938 was without parallel for so brief a period. National income fell 13 per cent, industrial production 33 per cent, payrolls 35 per cent, profits 78 per cent. Middle-class support for the President was severely strained.

Ironically the disaster struck just when the President was doing precisely what his middle-class followers had long urged: balancing the budget. Roosevelt had never been so wild a spender as his numerous business critics charged. Schooled in orthodox economics, he was uneasy about the mounting deficits and sensitive to charges that he lacked business sense. He also

ent shall incorporate the terms of this

ffecuated pursuant to Section 4 hereof,

ruary 28, 1938.

CARNEGIE-ILLINOIS STEEL CORPORATION,

By _____
                President.

STEEL WORKERS ORGANIZING COMMITTEE,

By _____
                Chairman.

_____
                Secretary-Treasurer

_____
                Director, Western Region

_____
                Director, Northeastern Region

_____
                General Counsel

The 1937 signing of this historic labor contract by Big Steel, long a leading foe of unionism, astounded everyone—including members of the steel workers union. They did not know that recently the company had been given reasonable assurance of fat British rearmament contracts—if it could guarantee uninterrupted production. It could—after signing up labor.

knew that it would be a fine thing politically to be able to report that the budget was balanced.

Toward this end, Roosevelt pushed ahead on a program of austerity early in 1937. He insisted on a severe slash in relief spending. A sharp cutback in federal outlays was accompanied by an increase in revenues. In 1937 the government collected two billion dollars in social security taxes, no part of which was disbursed; this money had come from the very groups most likely to spend. In 1936 the government had paid out a soldiers' bonus of $1.7 billion; in 1937 there was no comparable outlay. As a result, while the government had a large deficit in 1936, it actually had a cash surplus for 1937. Government spending no longer sparked the economy, and business failed to assume the initiative. By autumn Roosevelt was faced with a recession of disturbing proportions.

The events of 1937 pointed a lesson: that balancing the budget at a time of mass unemployment could have disastrous consequences. But it was a lesson both Roosevelt and most businessmen were slow to learn. Scared by the sudden downturn and excoriated by critics in business and industry, the President was more insistent than ever on balancing the budget. He sought ways to slash government spending and was angry at congressmen who wanted to spend without raising taxes.

Other forces were pulling the President in a different direction. Liberal leaders were voicing displeasure at the President's reliance on budget balancers like Secretary of the Treasury Henry Morgenthau Jr. In this influential coterie of Administration advisers were Harry Hopkins, Harold Ickes, social worker Aubrey Williams and Federal Reserve Chairman Marriner Eccles. They believed that when private investment declined, the government should step up spending. When a boom threatened to get out of hand, the government should slow it down by taxation. These New Dealers also believed the government should move vigorously to curb monopoly because they felt that the inflexible "administered" prices of the monopolies impeded the possibility of recovery.

A NUMBER of Roosevelt's advisers had been influenced by the British economist John Maynard Keynes. (Actually Keynes's influence on the New Deal was later exaggerated; he served largely to reinforce views the New Dealers already held.) Keynes had warned that a monthly deficit of $200 million would only work mischief, but that $400 million would take the country out of the Depression. Merely spending was no solution; it was necessary to spend *enough*. Keynes wrote to Roosevelt, urging him to take action to step up investment in durable goods like housing, public utilities and railroads. He thought Roosevelt's handling of housing had been "really wicked": construction, he argued, offered the best hope of recovery. "I should advise putting most of your eggs in this basket, *caring* about this more than anything, and making absolutely sure that they are being hatched without delay."

There was much to be said for public ownership of railroads and utilities, Keynes thought, but the important thing was to make a firm decision. If Roosevelt did not intend to nationalize, "what is the object of chasing the utilities round the lot every other week?" The President should either decide to nationalize or forget about past grievances and extend a helping hand. "To an Englishman," Keynes remarked, "you Americans, like the Irish, are

Sit-down strikers relax on auto seats in General Motors' Flint plant in 1937. Sit-downers observed a rigid code of behavior set by their union: no drinking, no property damage and no women in the plant. Kangaroo courts, held by respected workers, meted out punishments, ranging from small fines to the harsh penalty—for sit-downers—of expulsion from the plant.

At 24, James B. Carey of the Electrical Workers was the nation's youngest union president; at 27 he was sharp-tongued secretary of the CIO. Such was his reputation for militant unionism that when he sent an industrialist a box of cigars, the tycoon's secretary fearfully dumped them in a pail of water.

Among lusty trade unionists the teetotaling Walter Reuther of the Auto Workers was considered an anomaly. When he ran for the union presidency he said he would have a drink and a smoke if he won. Victorious, he gamely downed a shot of whiskey and smoked a cigarette, coughing and gagging.

so terribly historically-minded." Roosevelt, unimpressed, turned Keynes's thoughtful letter over to Morgenthau, Keynes's chief foe within the Administration, and the Secretary framed a deliberately noncommittal reply.

Critics of the New Deal had long argued that a time would come when the kind of improvisation to which Roosevelt had previously resorted would not suffice. The President would be forced to move in the direction of national planning, perhaps even toward the nationalization of basic industries. Or he would have to devise some way to take over a larger share of the decision-making on investment which now rested in the hands of a few corporation executives. Or he would have to commit the government to a vast program of deficit spending to encourage industrial revival. If he did not embrace any of these proposals, he would have to admit frankly that he was placing all his hopes on the initiative of businessmen and develop measures to restore business confidence.

HAMMERED at from all sides, Roosevelt could not decide what course to take. He was irritated by the mounting criticism, particularly since he felt that there were major differences between the "Roosevelt recession" and the "Hoover depression." The banks were now safe, the farmers could count on price supports, the jobless received relief. As the President told Congress: "All we need today is to look upon the fundamental, sound economic conditions to know that this business recession causes more perplexity than fear on the part of most people, and to contrast our prevailing mental attitude with the terror and despair of five years ago."

But the recession was taking a toll. By early 1938 one sixth of New York City was on relief; by spring, one third of Akron. The layoffs in the auto industry hit Middle Western industrial cities severely; in six months WPA rolls increased 434 per cent in Detroit, 571 per cent in Flint. WPA quotas were quickly filled, and once more the country went back to the dole. But the federal dole could not take care of everyone. When the Ohio legislature refused to vote relief funds, 65,000 people in Cleveland were deprived of a chief source of food and clothing. A social worker noted: "The grocers in poor neighborhoods have been closing down their shops. They say they cannot bear to refuse food to the families if they stay open."

Roosevelt recognized that action had to be taken. On April 2, 1938, the President announced he had decided on a government spending plan. A short time later Roosevelt asked Congress to approve a large-scale "lend-spend" program. He got nearly one billion dollars for public works and almost three billion dollars more for other federal activities. Yet, while the conservatives censured him for spending such gigantic sums, by Keynesian definitions the President was still not spending enough to make a decisive change in the economy. The initiative for getting out of the recession was still left with business.

Two weeks after Roosevelt sent his lend-spend message to Congress, he endorsed another recommendation of his liberal advisers: an investigation of the concentration of economic power. "Among us today," the President warned, "a concentration of private power without equal in history is growing. . . . Private enterprise is ceasing to be free enterprise and is becoming a cluster of private collectivisms: masking itself as a system of free enterprise after the American model, it is in fact becoming a concealed cartel system after the European model." Roosevelt declared that "the power of a few to manage the economic life of the nation must be diffused among the many or transferred to the public and its democratically responsible government." The President's search for a new antitrust policy, coming at a time when Roosevelt was under attack for failure to achieve recovery, served to deflect blame from his Administration by examining the sins of monopoly.

Congress agreed to the President's request for a full-dress investigation of monopoly and created the Temporary National Economic Committee, composed half of congressmen, half of Administration officials. The hearings of the TNEC marked the eclipse of lawyers and businessmen as experts on the state of the economy and the coming-of-age of the professional economist. Corporation attorneys found themselves bested by government economists, and most business leaders were revealed as parochial men who knew the technical details of their own industry but could not think of the problems of the economy as a whole. Business found it lacked the staffs of economists to do battle with the brain trusters.

Roosevelt's appointment in 1938 of the Yale Law School professor Thurman Arnold as Assistant Attorney General in charge of the Antitrust Division gave the foes of monopoly more to cheer about. Arnold enforced the antitrust laws with unusual vigor. He felt that the concentration of industry had done great economic damage by restricting production, thus depriving the public of benefits to which it was entitled. Even more ominous, cartelization threatened democracy. The centralized organization of German industry, Arnold noted, had created a perfect springboard for Hitler's leap to power.

In Arnold's five years in office he instituted 44 per cent of all the antitrust actions undertaken by the Justice Department since the passage of the Sherman Act in 1890. From July 1939 to July 1940 alone, Arnold's division secured judgments returning almost $2.7 million in fines to the Treasury. But Arnold also encountered a number of adverse court decisions, and when the country began to look to the large corporations to speed defense mobilization, the antimonopoly program lost much of its appeal. Despite his energetic administration of the antitrust laws, Arnold could claim few substantive gains.

"Pins and Needles," the topical review put on in this theater in 1937 by members of the Garment Workers, was the first Broadway hit with a union label. First intended as a weekend diversion, it drew rave reviews, ran four years (a record at the time) and gave a command performance in the White House.

BY 1938 the Roosevelt Administration no longer had its original exuberance or sense of direction. The New Deal had achieved much, but it had not ended unemployment. Some 10 million Americans were still out of work. In California the liberal Democratic Governor Culbert Olson expressed the belief of many when he questioned whether "the unemployed portion of our citizens will ever be wholly absorbed by private industry." The WPA continued to meet some of the needs of the jobless, but many states failed to respond with matching programs.

The persistence of the recession despite all of Roosevelt's efforts also cost him dear politically. In the fall of 1937 Southern Democrats and Republicans forged a coalition that would strongly affect American politics for the next generation. Democrats like Josiah Bailey of North Carolina and Harry Byrd of Virginia, who had opposed many of Roosevelt's policies, seized on the discontent in Congress to press for further budget balancing and to mobilize to wrest control of the party from the New Dealers at the 1940 convention. In the fall of 1937 a special session of Congress adjourned without passing a single measure Roosevelt had requested.

Early in 1938 the antagonism between President Roosevelt and the new

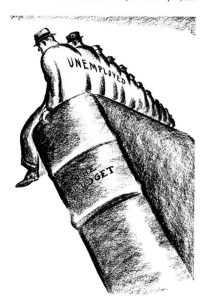

Two cartoons by Daniel Fitzpatrick of the St. Louis "Post-Dispatch" deal with the nagging problems of joblessness and low pay. Above, jobs and wages lag after rising production; below, unemployment unbalances the budget. Though corporations in 1936 showed a five billion dollar profit (after a two billion dollar loss in 1932) more than nine million stayed unemployed.

conservative coalition came to a head over the most unlikely issue anyone could have anticipated—the dull question of government reorganization. Both Presidents Taft and Hoover had favored executive reorganization, and when Franklin Roosevelt submitted a carefully drafted plan for reorganization of the executive branch of the government early in 1937, the proposal engendered relatively little controversy. But having tasted blood in the Supreme Court fight, Roosevelt's opponents saw in the reorganization bill a new opportunity to depict the President as a would-be dictator. One congressman described the measure as "a part of the great totalitarian movement that is developing over the world and is now sweeping over our borders." Bewildered by the turn of events, Roosevelt acted in a panicky fashion. He summoned newspapermen to a midnight conference to assure them he had no desire to be a dictator. But this move too backfired. Republicans said that he had called reporters for an "eerie midnight performance."

No attempt to appease the opposition with concessions did any good. On April 8, 1938, the House rejected the reorganization bill; when the vote was announced, the representatives cheered wildly. "Jim," the President said afterward to Farley, "I'll tell you that I didn't expect that vote. I can't understand it. There wasn't a chance for anyone to become a dictator under that bill."

ONCE the Roosevelt Revolution had lost its momentum, the forces of resistance to change made themselves felt in a number of ways. None was more mischievous than the Dies Committee. Some of the same critics who charged the President was a potential Fascist simultaneously accused him of fostering a Communist conspiracy. When the House Committee on Un-American Activities was created in 1938, it was intended to conduct a nonpartisan investigation of subversion. But under the chairmanship of the Texas Democrat Martin Dies, the committee became a forum for right-wing assaults on the Administration. Just when the Communists were attacking Roosevelt as a warmonger, Dies was insisting, "Stalin baited his hook with a 'progressive' worm, and New Deal suckers swallowed bait, hook, line, and sinker."

Not all of the committee's charges were wide of the mark. Communists certainly were influential in the Federal Theatre Project, for example. Outside of government they won control of some CIO unions, infiltrated youth groups and peace organizations, and achieved some influence on university campuses and in Hollywood.

Yet the influence of Communism was never great. Many intellectuals were annoyed by the bad-tempered dogmatism of the Communists; some, like John Dewey and Sinclair Lewis, were outspoken in their denunciation. Within the Administration no Communist had a decisive role in any important policy question or in shaping a single piece of legislation in the New Deal years. But foes of the Administration were able to use the Communist issue to drive another wedge into the Roosevelt coalition.

The New Dealers were especially exasperated by the rebuffs of the post-1936 period because they felt that the congressmen who were responsible did not reflect popular sentiment. This belief was reinforced by the congressional history of a wages-and-hours bill in 1937 and 1938. The bill, introduced in May 1937 by Senator Hugo Black, had met vigorous opposition from other Southern Democrats, who bottled it up in the House Rules Committee. A petition of House members might have brought it to a vote, but liberals could not win enough signatures. Then on May 3, 1938, the situation changed dramatically. In Florida's senatorial primary Claude Pepper, like Black a Southerner of liberal views, defeated an anti-New Deal congressman. Three days later a new petition on the wages-and-hours bill was swiftly signed by sufficient names; by mid-June Congress had enacted the Fair Labor Standards Act, which placed a floor under wages and a ceiling upon hours and wiped out child labor in industries in interstate commerce.

New Dealers were quick to conclude that the country still backed Roosevelt's policies; it was conservative congressmen who were out of step. They were particularly vexed by Democratic senators who had ridden into office on the President's popularity, only to oppose him once they had been elected. They were sure that if they went to the people and pointed out the record of these anti-New Deal Democrats, the people would respond by ousting the conservatives and electing men like Claude Pepper of Florida.

On June 24, 1938, the President declared that he would intervene in certain Democratic primaries in order to defeat anti-Administration lawmakers. "Never in our lifetime," he said, "has such a concerted campaign of defeatism been thrown at the heads of the President and Senators and Congressmen as in the case of this 75th Congress." As leader of a party dedicated to liberal principles, he stated: "I feel that I have every right to speak in those few instances where there may be a clear issue between candidates for a Democratic nomination involving these principles or involving a clear misuse of my name."

Hastily the White House organized a campaign to "purge" a number of legislators, notably Senators Walter George in Georgia, Cotton Ed Smith in South Carolina and Millard Tydings in Maryland. Roosevelt toured the country, but the campaign never got off the ground. The New Dealers unseated a congressman in New York City; elsewhere Roosevelt took a drubbing. He did not dare to oppose some of the most adamantly anti-New Deal senators, and those he did combat—George, Smith and Tydings—all won re-election.

Roosevelt came out of the purge experience badly hurt. Two years later, when Senator Harry Truman asked Roosevelt's aid in a primary fight in Missouri, a White House secretary primly informed a Truman supporter that it was the President's "invariable practice" to take no part in primaries.

Instead of getting a more favorable Congress in the 1938 elections, Roosevelt found one that was even more opposed to his programs. The Republicans picked up 81 seats in the House and eight in the Senate. In the process the G.O.P. introduced to the country a new senator from Ohio, Robert Taft, and a 31-year-old Governor of Minnesota named Harold Stassen—and made a major political figure of the 36-year-old racket-busting district attorney Thomas Dewey, who had come within a few votes of ousting Herbert Lehman as governor of New York.

AFTER 1938 Roosevelt failed to win even one major piece of reform legislation. In his annual message to Congress in January 1939, the President, for the first time, proposed no new measures. "We have now passed the period of internal conflict in the launching of our program of social reforms," he told Congress. "Our full energies may now be released to invigorate the processes of recovery in order to preserve our reforms." By 1939 Roosevelt was compelled to direct much of his attention to problems of foreign policy; most of his later successes were to be won in this field. The New Deal was at an end.

Republican Robert A. Taft, a new face in the 1939 Senate, had simple tastes. Once when he left a Washington dinner the doorman shouted, "Senator Taft's car!" Taft, one of the few guests without a chauffeur, murmured: "Well, it's a good car, but it won't come when it's called." He got his Dodge himself.

Harold E. Stassen was a veteran politician at 31 when he hit the G.O.P. big time as Minnesota governor in 1939. He had been a county attorney at 23. Even before, while at the University of Minnesota, he was so active in politics that he had to hire a fraternity mate to be his personal secretary.

F.D.R.—grand master of politics

FRANKLIN D. ROOSEVELT was a rich man's son, a graduate of Groton and Harvard, a stiff-necked youth who seemed an unlikely candidate for the business of politics. Yet he enjoyed not one but two separate political careers. In 1910, when he was 28, Dutchess County Democratic leaders in New York thought he had a chance to win the race for state senator. But when he dropped by headquarters in riding clothes, they had their doubts. One politician said: "You'll have to take off those yellow shoes and put on pants." He ran, campaigning in an open red Maxwell, and surprisingly, he won.

But his career was cut short in 1921 when he was stricken with polio. For three years he battled to overcome the effects of the disease. In 1924, crippled for life, he re-entered politics with a speech nominating Al Smith for President. Smith lost the nomination, but the speech made F.D.R. In the following years he became governor of New York; then he ran for and won the presidency. By now he was a confident, aggressive leader, daunted by nothing. But the night after his election he told his son James: "All my life I have been afraid of only one thing—fire. Tonight I think I'm afraid of something else . . . that I may not have the strength to do this job." Four months later he was inaugurated President of the United States (opposite), and he went on to do the job for 12 years, longer than any other man in U.S. history.

IN THE 1924 CAMPAIGN Roosevelt is visited at Hyde Park by (from left) Lieutenant Governor G. R. Lunn, presidential candidate John W. Davis and Governor Alfred E. Smith. That year F.D.R., in delivering a speech that nominated Smith as the "Happy Warrior," made himself a power in the Democratic party.

ON THE PLATFORM in Covarrubias' caricature of the 1933 inauguration are (from left) ex-Vice President Curtis, Mrs. Hoover, Herbert Hoover, Vice President Garner, Mrs. Roosevelt, F.D.R. and Chief Justice Hughes. Below at rear are Senator Joe Robinson, Raymond Moley, General Pershing; at center Al Smith, Jim Farley; in front Mark Sullivan, Walter Lippmann and Louis Howe.

AS AN ADMINISTRATOR, Assistant Secretary of the Navy Roosevelt *(left)* inspects a World War I seaplane. He held the post under Wilson from 1913 to 1920, did much to prepare the Navy for waging war—and learned a lot about Washington.

AS A CANDIDATE for Vice Preside[nt] in 1920, Roosevelt marches in D[ay]ton, Ohio, with James M. Cox, t[he] head of the ticket. They lost t[he] election, but F.D.R. later declare[d] "I got to know the country as o[nly] . . . a traveling salesman ca[n]

The "mean cuss" who became an irresistible winner

YOU know, I was an awfully mean cuss when I first went into politics," Roosevelt recalled in later life. As a young man he antagonized strangers by looking down his nose through gold pince-nez. "Awful arrogant fellow, that Roosevelt," one Tammany veteran said.

Roosevelt changed. Friends said that his battle with paralysis had broadened him, enemies that his charm was hypocrisy. But no one denied that it worked. For millions of voters of the '30s, the familiar tossed-back head and the gleaming Roosevelt grin were symbols of courage as heartening as the words of his first inaugural: "This great Nation . . . will revive and will prosper."

THE PUBLIC'S F.D.R. throws back his head and cocks his cigarette holder skyward in a famous pose. He liked to drive himself whenever possible; his cars had special hand controls.

THE REPORTERS' F.D.R. holds his first White House press conference in March 1933. Through these conferences and radio talks, he molded public opinion as no one had before him.

IN NEBRASKA Mrs. Roosevelt tours with her husband in 1935. Her rules for herself on campaign trips included: "Do as little talking as humanly possible. . . . Be sure not to get too fat."

IN OHIO Mrs. Roosevelt visits a coal mine in 1935. Her reluctance to travel with guards alarmed the Secret Service. She finally agreed to carry her own pistol—and became a good shot.

The President's eyes and ears: "My Missus"

BACK HOME, "Babs" (as F.D.R. called her) receives a warm embrace. The two generally ate by themselves on her first evening home from a jaunt, so she could brief him fully on her findings.

FOR Gosh sakes, here comes Mrs. Roosevelt," one astonished coal miner exclaimed to another in a cartoon Robert Day drew for *The New Yorker* in 1933. The fact is, Eleanor Roosevelt turned up in coal mines twice—in West Virginia in 1933 and two years later in Ohio (*above*). Her travels as First Lady were a source of countless "Eleanor jokes," but her reports on her trips helped keep the President informed; and when he quoted her opinions at Cabinet meetings ("My Missus says . . ."), he was not fooling. James Farley, himself a consummate politician, called her "the most practical woman I've ever met in politics."

If it had not been for Mrs. Roosevelt, F.D.R. might never have become President. During the years of his illness, she had struggled against the determination of her mother-in-law, Sara Delano Roosevelt, to prevent Franklin's return to politics. Eleanor won; she was far more tough-fibered than she appeared. "I always looked at everything from the point of view of what I *ought* to do, rarely from what I wanted to do," she once said.

Her fight for the humanitarian causes she believed in went on after her husband's death. From 1946 to 1953, and again in 1961, she served as a member of the U.S. delegation to the United Nations. When she died at 78 in 1962, she was mourned at home and abroad as "First Lady of the world," a towering figure in her own right.

Mrs. Roosevelt entertains troops at the White House in 1942. Her gift, one said, was to make each feel she was "here just to talk to you."

Roosevelt visits Pierre, South Dakota, in 1935. For F.D.R. every trip was a campaign tour. "He liked going around the country," Frances

A nation and a man on a "rendezvous with destiny"

THERE have been many explanations for Franklin Roosevelt's political success, some idolatrous, some libelous. He had loyal aides around him and political machines behind him. He enjoyed juggling politicians, and he did it so adroitly that often they did not realize until later what had happened to them.

Above all, Roosevelt could speak to Americans as no one else could. Before inspiring the nation in wartime,

WITH HIS RUNNING MATES, F.D.R. shares the spotlight with three vice presidents. Above, "Cactus Jack" Garner and Roosevelt celebrate renomination at the 1936 convention. In 1940 Roosevelt's insistence on Henry A. Wallace *(left)*, angered party regulars, who considered him a dangerous maverick. For 1944 his running mate was Missouri's Harry S. Truman *(opposite)*, best known as a Senate investigator.

Perkins recalled. "His personal relationship with crowds was on a warm, simple level of a friendly, neighborly exchange of affection."

he lifted it from apathy and despair in the Great Depression. "I pledge you, I pledge myself, to a new deal for the American people," he said, accepting the 1932 nomination. His optimism was electric. "This generation of Americans has a rendezvous with destiny," he said in accepting his second nomination; the words thrilled millions. His humor could be devastating, as he demonstrated when he turned the names of three political opponents—"a perfectly beautiful rhythm, Congressmen Martin, Barton and Fish"—into a campaign chant that delighted partisan audiences in 1940. His touch was unerring. Once an aide wrote a speech that ended:"We are trying to construct a more inclusive society." Roosevelt rewrote the last line—and in the process touched the hearts of Americans everywhere: "We are going to make a country in which no one is left out."

IN THE WHITE HOUSE Roosevelt traces the grim course of the Pacific war while broadcasting a fireside chat in February 1942. Singapore had fallen a week before; the Japanese were within striking distance of Australia; as he spoke, an enemy submarine lobbed shells onto the California shore. But F.D.R. promised: "Soon we and not our enemies will have the offensive."

A wartime leader with a glowing vision of peace

THE war made Roosevelt a campaigner on a global scale—a campaigner for military victory and for a world organization to guarantee the peace that would follow. He had witnessed Woodrow Wilson's failure after World War I, but he believed he could prevail. Cockily he said of Stalin: "I can handle the old buzzard."

He traveled as no President ever had before—by warship and by air (in his C-54, the *Sacred Cow*)—working his personal diplomacy upon the leaders of nations. And highly personal it was. "I'm a tree farmer," he greeted Ibn Saud at one conference, presumably baffling that monarch, who knew nothing of Hyde Park's stand of Christmas trees. He seldom meddled in tactical military decisions, but at one meeting when a New Zealand expert recommended taking a particular Pacific island, Roosevelt interrupted. "No," he said, "Mangareva would be better." The expert had never heard of it. "Oh, it's in the Tuamotu Archipelago, in the postal administration of Tahiti," said F.D.R. "I'm a stamp collector."

IN CAIRO Roosevelt meets Generalissimo and Madame Chiang Kai-shek in November 1943. Chinese hopes for a major Southeast Asia campaign were to be disappointed.

ON A CRUISER, the *Quincy*, in Egypt's Great Bitter Lake, F.D.R. and King Farouk confer during the February 1945 "Conference with the Three Kings." (The other two were Ibn Saud and Haile Selassie.)

IN SICILY F.D.R. reviews troops in December 1943. He had just set the Normandy invasion date with Churchill and Stalin at Teheran and told Eisenhower he was to be commander.

NEAR EXHAUSTION, but eager to scotch rumors about his health, F.D.R. rides in an open car through a cold October rain after making a 1944 campaign speech in New York.

At the gates of victory, sudden death

On March 1, 1945, Franklin Roosevelt reported to a joint session of Congress (*left*) on his trip to Yalta. His audience was shocked. Suddenly, at 63, F.D.R. appeared terribly old. Only a few months before, he had insisted on driving more than 50 miles in an open car (*above*), through four New York City boroughs, in weather that drove younger men indoors. Now he was clearly in poor health. He sat, as he never had, while addressing Congress, and his voice was thin and hurried.

The end came on April 12, 1945, at Warm Springs, Georgia, of a cerebral hemorrhage. When the news struck, millions of Americans, feeling their hearts skip a beat, told one another that the world would never be the same without him.

89

5. ON THE WORLD STAGE

IN his annual message to Congress on January 3, 1936, Franklin Roosevelt recalled that in his inaugural address three years before he had been able to limit his comments on foreign affairs to a single paragraph. If he were to deliver that inaugural address now, he observed, he would be compelled to devote the greater part to world affairs. As Roosevelt spoke, planes of the Italian dictator Benito Mussolini were bombing Ethiopians, Adolf Hitler was readying his bold march into the Rhineland and Japanese militarists were hatching plans for a "New Order in Greater East Asia."

Even before Roosevelt took office the post-Versailles world was collapsing. The Great Depression, which had helped bring Adolf Hitler to power as the Führer in Germany and encourage the militarists in Japan, had weakened the democracies' will to resist. In America isolationism became a kind of national secular religion in the 1930s. The desire to immunize America from Europe's quarrels was ancient doctrine, but it had developed new vigor from the bitter memories of World War I. In the United States and in Western Europe, entreaties to organize collective measures to forestall the Fascists fell on deaf ears because they sounded so much like the sloganeering of World War I.

Disillusionment with World War I not only strengthened the convictions of the isolationists but nourished a pacifist movement that won millions of adherents. Some colleges which had military training abolished it. Princeton students burlesqued the nation's veterans' organizations by forming the

ABSOLUTE MASTER of Germany, Adolf Hitler gives the Nazi salute at a 1938 parade. That year he annexed Austria and the Sudetenland, pushing Europe nearer to war.

Veterans of Future Wars and asking Congress for bonuses for future military service so they could spend the money while they were still alive.

Isolationism in the 1930s was strengthened by the belief of many Americans that the Versailles Treaty was a grossly unfair settlement. In this atmosphere the Fascist powers were able to win a good deal of sympathy by making themselves out to be "have-not" countries whose only demand was enough living space for their people; if the "have" nations would surrender some of their holdings there would be no need of conquest.

In the 1940 movie "The Great Dictator," Charlie Chaplin ridiculed Hitler's dream of world conquest. Chaplin played the part of Adenoid Hynkel, Jack Oakie the role of his strutting Axis partner, Benzino Napaloni. The film produced strong but mixed reactions. It was banned in Eire and Brazil in deference to the Axis, but it was a smash hit in wartime Britain.

THE pressure of isolationist and pacifist opinion left President Roosevelt little room to maneuver. Even before he was nominated for the presidency, he had yielded to the demand of the publisher William Randolph Hearst that he publicly oppose American entrance into the League of Nations. When, in the spring of 1933, he made a modest proposal not to interfere with the League sanctions against an aggressor if the European powers would agree to a program of disarmament, isolationists in the Senate rebuffed him.

Since Roosevelt had served as Wilson's Assistant Secretary of the Navy and had campaigned for the vice presidency in 1920 as a Wilsonian internationalist, the leadership in Congress never quite trusted his apparent conversion to isolationism. Congress repeatedly tied his hands on foreign policy. As a result Roosevelt was reduced through most of his first two terms to moralizing gestures which proved futile in curbing the aggressors.

The leaders of the Western democracies faced three difficult tasks: to maintain peace, to contain Fascism and to restore the international economic community. As late as 1937 it was probably still possible to check Fascism without war, and the failure to do so must be charged largely to Britain and France. America's refusal to assume responsibility for the peace also had serious consequences, but this pattern had been established long before Roosevelt came to power, and he could do little to alter it. However, Roosevelt must shoulder much of the blame for the failure to achieve the third goal.

When Roosevelt took office he inherited a commitment from Hoover that the United States would take part in an international economic conference in London to deal with stabilization of world currency and reduction of trade barriers. The President thrilled the internationalists with a stirring message stressing the need for world economic co-operation. Secretary of State Hull, long a crusader for free trade, had high hopes for the London conference.

The conference convened on June 12, 1933, and from the first found itself in difficulties. Each country professed to favor the liberalization of trade, but none wanted to surrender special advantages. The American delegates were badly divided on policy; some were woefully ignorant of foreign affairs. Hull's position was pitiful. He could not offer tariff concessions because Roosevelt had refused to send the necessary reciprocal trade bill to Congress. He could not discuss war debts or reparations or stabilization. He could only express his earnest desire for freer trade and appear to some as a moralizing bumbler.

Although Roosevelt had forbidden the delegates to take up currency stabilization, several Treasury and banking experts had gone along to discuss temporary stabilization with the French and British. Roosevelt had urged such a program upon the world in May. But as rumors from London indicated an imminent stabilization agreement, security prices in New York broke and some commodity prices began to drop. Hugh Johnson protested to Raymond

Moley: "An agreement to stabilize now on the lines your boy friends in London are suggesting would bust to hell and gone the prices we're sweating to raise." Roosevelt vetoed the proposal and sent Moley to London. The most Moley would agree to was a harmless statement by the countries involved, promising they would do their best to stabilize currencies. But on July 3 Roosevelt fired a "bombshell" message to the conference which ended all hopes of economic co-operation. He not only repudiated Moley's position, but he scolded the other nations for failure to live within their means. The message, wrote Philip Snowden, former Chancellor of the Exchequer, "will be filed for all times as a classic example of conceit, hectoring and ambiguity."

Hull gained something more substantial the following year. Under the Trade Agreements Act of 1934, the President could raise or lower existing tariff rates up to 50 per cent for countries which would reciprocate with similar concessions for American products. The reciprocal trade agreements were touted as a notable victory for the internationalists. In fact, they produced meager results. They won some political good will, but they did not appreciably alter the enormous imbalance caused by the position of the United States as a creditor nation with a largely self-sufficient economy.

To the question of how to recover America's lost foreign trade, one practical answer was proposed: recognition of the Soviet Union. American exports to Russia had fallen from $114.4 million in 1930 to $12.6 million in 1932; most businessmen, politicians and editors argued that granting recognition would be an important step in regaining this market. Why, asked Hearst's New York *American,* "should the Government of this country . . . turn away hundreds of millions in real money that Russians are willing to spend?"

Roosevelt and Hull were less interested in the possibility of renewed trade than in the hope that the Soviet Union might be a stabilizing force in Europe and Asia. On November 16, 1933, the two countries formally resumed diplomatic relations. The Soviets promised to guarantee religious liberty to Americans in the U.S.S.R. and to curb Communist propaganda in the United States. Russia's World War I debt was left for future settlement.

As it turned out, recognition was an event of little consequence, either for good or for evil. There was only a modest increase in trade. In international affairs the U.S.S.R. proved unpredictable and made little effort to curb propaganda. On the other hand no harm resulted either; the United States had merely acknowledged what all other great powers had long since been forced to concede—that the Soviet state existed.

Hitler (left) and Mussolini, portrayed as twin Napoleons in this cartoon, were never really close friends. After their first meeting in 1934, Mussolini spoke of the new German chancellor with contempt, referring to him as a buffoon. After Italy collapsed in World War II, Hitler said that his relationship with the Duce "could be added to the list of my mistakes."

SHACKLED as he was by isolationists in Congress, Roosevelt was restricted to actions in foreign affairs which called for no new commitments in Europe. Soviet recognition was one such enterprise, the Good Neighbor Policy toward Latin America another. The first steps toward ending American interventionism south of the border had been taken under Coolidge and Hoover; the first months of Roosevelt's Administration actually were marked by a resurgence of the earlier policy of interference. The State Department's Sumner Welles persuaded Roosevelt to withhold recognition of a new revolutionary regime in Cuba and to assign no less than 30 ships to Cuban waters. But at the Seventh International Conference of American States in Montevideo in December 1933, the American delegation voted for a resolution that no state had the right to intervene in the affairs of another. A few days later

Roosevelt affirmed that "the definite policy of the United States from now on is one opposed to armed intervention."

Before the end of Roosevelt's first term, the United States had relinquished its legal right to intervene in Panama, the last Marines had left Haiti and a treaty with Cuba had ended the American protectorate of the island. Only the right to maintain a naval base at Guantánamo was retained.

Roosevelt's Good Neighbor Policy received its sternest test in 1938 when President Lázaro Cárdenas expropriated almost all the foreign-owned oil industry in Mexico. American oil companies tried to whip up support for an ultimatum to Mexico to return the oil properties. Roosevelt not only refused to intervene, but advised the oil companies to pare down their demands. A compromise settlement was finally reached in 1941.

It was not only the oil companies that found occasional fault with the Good Neighbor doctrine. Catholic leaders were concerned over anticlerical activities in Mexico. Liberals, who had long argued for a policy of nonintervention, were dismayed by the realization that this meant that Washington could do nothing to overturn dictators of the stripe of Rafael Trujillo in the Dominican Republic and Fulgencio Batista in Cuba.

Maxim Litvinov, the shrewd Soviet diplomat, favored co-operation with the democracies. Once his friendliness bordered on indiscretion: He told a reporter that if the U.S. bowed to Soviet demands it would simply lead "to the West being faced . . . with the next series of demands." The interview was sped to Washington and kept top secret until Litvinov died in 1951.

IN the Far East also Roosevelt had a much freer hand than in Europe. The American attitude toward the Orient was a curious compound of arrogance, missionary benevolence, fear of the "yellow peril," illusory hopes for more trade and sentimental concern for China. In 1940 Kenneth Wherry, later elected senator from Nebraska, told a cheering audience: "With God's help we will lift Shanghai up and up, ever up, until it is just like Kansas City."

From the Hoover Administration Roosevelt inherited both a policy and a problem with regard to Japan. When the Japanese began military operations in Manchuria in September 1931, they not only offered the first serious challenge to the Versailles Treaty structure, but aroused Hoover's Secretary of State, Henry L. Stimson, to state that America would not admit the legality of any situation which might impair the treaty rights of the United States. The "Stimson Doctrine," as this policy came to be known, had actually been suggested by President Hoover, but Hoover opposed implementing it with economic sanctions, a device Stimson had contemplated. So Japan was able to demonstrate to the world that it was possible to embark on a war of aggression and get away with it.

On January 9, 1933, Stimson met with President-elect Roosevelt at Hyde Park; a week later Roosevelt announced he supported Stimson's Far Eastern policy. Nevertheless, neither the President nor advisers such as Ambassador to Japan Joseph C. Grew really favored strong measures against Tokyo. American policy remained fundamentally isolationist.

American isolationism vis-à-vis the Far East as well as Europe was reinforced by the conviction that munitions makers had precipitated World War I and were intriguing to touch off a new arms race. As conservative a senator as Republican Arthur Vandenberg of Michigan denounced the arms traffic as "unutterable" treason and advocated confiscating virtually all income in excess of $10,000 in the event of war. In March 1934 FORTUNE published an influential article, "Arms and the Men," which charged that the German war drive in World War I had been maintained by weapons made in England and France. Disturbed by such reports on the international arms traffic, the Senate authorized a committee headed by Senator Gerald Nye of North Dakota to investigate the munitions industry.

The result of American war fears was a far-reaching measure defining American conduct in the event of a foreign war. The Neutrality Act of 1935 stipulated a mandatory embargo on implements of war to belligerents, forbade American ships to carry munitions to nations at war and empowered the President at his discretion to deny protection to American citizens traveling on belligerent ships. Six months later the Neutrality Act of 1936 extended the embargo and placed restrictions on loans to belligerents.

When Italian forces invaded Ethiopia in October 1935, Roosevelt found he had no effective way to check Mussolini. He was deterred not only by the neutrality legislation, but by politicians in both parties who feared to offend Italian-Americans. At a meeting of 10,000 in Boston, the Sons of Italy branded Britain "a disturber of world peace" for suggesting sanctions against Mussolini. When Generoso Pope of New York City, publisher of the Italian-language newspaper *Il Progresso*, called on the President, Roosevelt felt compelled to assure him: "Gene, America honestly wishes to remain neutral . . . tell the Italians, through your newspapers, that our neutrality will in no way imply discrimination at the expense of Italy and in favor of any other nation."

By the summer of 1936 the President seemed to have surrendered altogether to the isolationists and pacifists. In an address at Chautauqua, New York, in August 1936, he asserted: "We shun political commitments which might entangle us in foreign wars; we avoid connection with the political activities of the League of Nations. . . . I have seen war. I have seen war on land and sea. I have seen blood running from the wounded. . . . I have seen the agony of mothers and wives. I hate war."

After the Spanish Civil War started in 1936, Roosevelt outdid the isolationists in his reliance on neutrality legislation. On January 6, 1937, he asked the new Congress to amend the Neutrality Act "to cover specific points raised by the unfortunate civil strife in Spain." General Francisco Franco, leader of the Fascist rebels, said gratefully: "President Roosevelt behaved in the manner of a true gentleman."

As "volunteers" sent by Hitler and by Mussolini intervened in Spain (Ambassador William C. Bullitt reported from Paris that Italians in Franco's army outnumbered Spaniards 3 to 1), it became increasingly clear that the Fascist powers were raising a direct challenge to democracy. But Secretary of State Hull insisted that the United States must support Neville Chamberlain, who became British prime minister in 1937, in seeking to prevent the spread of war to the rest of Europe. Hull and Ambassador to Britain Joseph P. Kennedy persuaded the President that lifting the arms embargo would be resented by Britain and might extend the conflict.

The weakness of the democracies in the face of aggression in Spain convinced the Fascists that they had little to fear when they launched their next offensive. "My own impression," wrote Ambassador Claude Bowers prophetically from Madrid in July 1937, "is that with every surrender beginning long ago with China, followed by Abyssinia [Ethiopia] and then Spain, the Fascist powers, with vanity inflamed, will turn without delay to some other country —such as Czechoslovakia—and that with every surrender the prospects of a European war grow darker."

Although Ambassador to Tokyo Joseph Grew unerringly predicted the Japanese attack on Hawaii and was outraged by incidents like the 1941 bombing of the U.S. gunboat "Tutuila," he hoped for years that it would be possible to stave off war with Japan. A more realistic Harvard man, F.D.R., once told the diplomat, "Joe, the only trouble with you is you're too darn nice."

Joseph P. Kennedy, ambassador to Britain, collected much useful information from his children traveling in Europe In 1939 he received a long letter about the tension between Poland and Germany. It reported an impression that "the Poles will fight over the Question of Danzig." Kennedy's informant was the future President of the U.S., his son John F., then 21.

In 1937 Congress extended the arms embargo and the ban on loans to include civil conflicts. However, fearing that a total embargo would cripple the economy, Congress worked out the compromise of "cash-and-carry": belligerents could buy goods (excluding munitions) in the United States if they paid for them on delivery and hauled them away in foreign ships.

By the time Roosevelt signed this Neutrality Act of 1937, he was a troubled man. Deeply alarmed by the menace of Hitler and by the potential threat of Japan, he was looking for some way that would both preserve peace and support those elements in Britain and France which were attempting to curb Fascist aggression. In October 1937, in an address in Chicago, Roosevelt sought to alert the country to the peril it faced. He warned that "the epidemic of world lawlessness" was spreading and added: "When an epidemic of physical disease starts to spread, the community approves and joins in a quarantine of the patients in order to protect the health of the community. . . ." The President's "quarantine" speech was interpreted as a new turn in his foreign policy—the abandonment of isolation for collective security and advance notice to Tokyo of sanctions against Japan.

But the extent to which the United States was still following an isolationist line quickly became apparent. The day after Roosevelt's talk the League of Nations Assembly proposed a conference in Brussels to consider action against Japan. The conference was a dismal failure. Japan did not even attend, the United States delegate was instructed not to make any kind of commitment and the other nations barely went through the motions of considering action.

Three weeks later Japanese war planes bombed and sank the gunboat U.S.S. *Panay* in the Yangtze River in China. Two Americans died, 14 were wounded. Though some congressmen were indignant, most seemed to feel that the solution was to have the United States pull out of the Orient. In any case, at this point Japan was as anxious to avoid trouble as the United States was. Foreign Minister Hirota hurried to the American embassy in Tokyo to express the profound apologies of his government, and Japan closed the affair with a check for $2,214,007.36, which met American claims to the last penny.

FOR the moment a showdown had been averted. George Fielding Eliot, the military commentator, wrote in 1938 that it was "absurd" to think Japan would fight America. He added that "a Japanese attack upon Hawaii is a strategical impossibility." Yet by mid-1938 Ambassador Grew was alarmed by increasing signs of a war psychology in Japan. An ardent golfer, he noted the disappearance of rubber golf balls from the market—a clear indication, he felt, that Nippon was tightening its belt "for a long pull." The tone of Japanese statements was changing too. Tokyo now bluntly declared that it was building a New Order in East Asia in which Japan would have a preferential position.

In Europe the Fascist powers were on the march. Hitler occupied Austria in March 1938. In September there was near-panic as the Nazi leader demanded that Czechoslovakia hand over to Germany its Sudeten region, populated largely by Germans. As the Czechs prepared to fight, their British and French allies, in the persons of Prime Minister Chamberlain and Premier Daladier, met with Hitler at Munich and acceded abjectly to his demands.

The Munich crisis broke American complacency about events in Europe. The nation was held spellbound by radio reports. For 20 days H. V. Kaltenborn virtually lived in the studios; he broadcast 102 times. By the end of the month America had a new pastime—turning on the radio to hear analyses from New York, Washington and foreign capitals of perplexing world news.

In November 1938, as retaliation for the murder of a minor German diplomatic official in Paris, the Nazis carried out a vast pogrom against Jews in Germany. The number of Jews and other opponents of Fascism who fled to America—a list which already included such notables as the physicist Albert Einstein and the novelist Thomas Mann—increased sharply. Yet the United States had little reason for pride in its policy toward the refugees. Its immigration quotas barred many later murdered by Hitler.

NOWHERE did there seem to be the will to resist the Fascist powers. Chamberlain's foreign secretary Anthony Eden, who opposed appeasing Hitler and Mussolini, resigned; Eden's departure helped convince many Americans that Britain had deserted the democratic cause and that the United States must withdraw still further from European power politics.

Roosevelt responded to the threat posed by Fascist expansion by stepping up American rearmament. He conferred with General of the Armies John J. Pershing, commander in chief of the A.E.F. in World War I, on plans to strengthen the Army, which was smaller at the time than the Greek or Bulgarian armies (including reserves) and woefully ill-equipped. He also asked for the greatest naval construction program since World War I. "The two madmen," he later explained, "respect force and force alone." Congress voted Roosevelt increased military and naval appropriations, but isolationists denounced the President as a warmonger who was manufacturing a crisis.

There were still many Americans who thought Hitler's demands were reasonable. The German leader soon disabused most of them of this notion. In September 1938 the Führer had said that once the Sudeten question was settled, there would be "no further territorial problems in Europe." He added: "We do not want any Czechs." Less than six months later Hitler gobbled up most of the rest of Czechoslovakia. In that single stroke he rendered general war all but inevitable. Two weeks later Chamberlain, finally disillusioned with appeasement, announced that Britain and France would go to the aid of Poland—now under increasing German pressure—if the Poles were forced to fight to keep their independence.

During the same month that Hitler seized Czechoslovakia, German troops also entered Memel, an autonomous territory on the coast of Lithuania, while Japan claimed the Spratly Islands southwest of Manila and Franco captured Madrid. Ten days after Franco's conquest Mussolini seized Albania. "Never in my life," Roosevelt wrote, "have I seen things moving in the world with more cross currents or with greater velocity." In April 1939 he said he had been told that there was an even chance of war in Europe and that it was even money which side would win. He commented that the totalitarian countries could get 1,500 aircraft into South America overnight: "We have 80 planes that could get there in time to meet them."

That spring Great Britain set about to win the good will of the United States in the impending conflict: King George VI and Queen Elizabeth visited North America. The king tolerated a slap on the back from Vice President Garner, placed a wreath on Washington's tomb and rode around the grounds of the World's Fair in New York in a miniature train. The royal couple spent their last day in the United States picnicking with the Roosevelts at Hyde

Foreign Minister Anthony Eden (right) resigned in 1938 after many disagreements with Prime Minister Neville Chamberlain (left). Here both men are seen in the fall of 1937 when Eden was urging that British rearming be speeded to meet the menace of Germany and Italy. Chamberlain refused to listen, and once told Eden to "go home and take an aspirin."

Running for the G.O.P. nomination, Wendell Willkie made a very important speech in St. Paul. His prepared address received only polite applause. Faced with disaster, Willkie tossed the pages into the air and said: "Some damn fool told me I had to read a speech to you. Now let me tell you what I really think." As he finished, 700 Republicans arose yelling "More! More!"

Park. The king took off his necktie and, it was widely noted, ate hot dogs.

Three months later Britain was at war. On Sunday morning, September 3, in response to the German invasion of Poland two days before, Chamberlain told the British people that their country was at war with the Third Reich. Three weeks after that the President asked a special session of Congress to repeal the arms embargo. Of the Neutrality Act of 1935 he now said: "I regret that the Congress passed that Act. I regret equally that I signed that Act."

After six weeks of heated debate, Roosevelt got repeal of the arms embargo and the application of cash-and-carry to munitions as well as raw materials. But American ships might not sail to belligerent ports and could be forbidden to enter combat zones. When on November 4 Roosevelt defined the entire Baltic plus the Atlantic from northern Spain to southern Norway as a combat zone, one writer noted that American vessels had been removed from the seas "as effectively as if all our ships had been torpedoed."

IN the 1930s some Americans had supported Communist causes in the belief that Soviet Russia was a determined foe of Fascism and imperialism. In 1939 that illusion was shattered for most of them. A Nazi-Soviet pact of non-aggression in August 1939 had freed Hitler to launch World War II. Then, shortly after German armies invaded Poland from the west, Russian forces drove into the nation from the east. On November 30 the Red army crossed the border of Finland. The Russians treated all protests with arrogant disdain.

Save for the Communists, Americans were united in sympathy for Finland. Harold Ickes, who had often been accused by extremists of being sympathetic to Communism, called the attack on Finland an assault by "Russian barbarians" and added: "Stalin is more than out-Hitlering Hitler." Yet the United States was still so wedded to isolationism that Congress would not vote a penny in military aid for the Finns. A small credit was finally approved for nonmilitary materials, but by then the Finns were seeking an armistice.

In Western Europe the war had apparently settled down to a long stalemate. It seemed that the Germans could not pierce France's concrete wall, the Maginot Line, that Britain's control of the seas would eventually insure an Allied victory, and that the United States, without danger to itself, could be the quartermaster for the Allied forces. Most Americans saw no need to get more deeply involved.

At dawn on April 9, 1940, Hitler's troops crossed the border of Denmark. Almost simultaneously thousands of German troops began landing on the coast of Norway. Denmark fell in hours, Norway in nine weeks. On May 10 the Nazis swarmed through the Low Countries. The Netherlands was overrun in five days, Belgium in 18. In only a little more than three weeks, the Nazis drove the British armies out of France, and the Panzer divisions outflanked the Maginot Line. On June 22 the Third French Republic surrendered to Hitler.

Americans were stunned. It had taken less than three months to destroy their illusions about the outcome of the European war and their own impregnability. Walter Lippmann wrote: "Our duty is to begin acting at once on the basic assumption that . . . before the snow flies again we may stand alone and isolated, the last great Democracy on earth."

For the moment, even Roosevelt's severest critics rallied to him as the national leader in a time of crisis. He called for a vast increase in armaments and moved to create a crisis government of national unity. On June 19 he named two prominent Republicans to the chief defense posts in his cabinet: Henry Stimson as Secretary of War and Frank Knox as Secretary of the Navy.

Roosevelt had hoped Mussolini might be used as a counter against Hitler, but that month Italy declared war on France and Britain. Fighting mad, Roosevelt ad libbed a burning sentence: "On this tenth day of June, 1940, the hand that held the dagger has struck it into the back of its neighbor."

Although Roosevelt was convinced that aid to Britain was America's first line of defense, it was not clear what aid the United States could give. The nation did not have enough planes for even its own minimal requirements; the American Army was that of a third-class power; the Navy was committed to the Pacific. Moreover, many believed that Britain had only a slim chance for survival. One American diplomat noted that Ambassador Kennedy was "quite a realist, and he sees England gone."

Nonetheless Roosevelt pushed on with aid to Britain. He released Navy planes to be sold to the Allies and made available more than 500,000 Lee-Enfield rifles, as well as machine guns, ammunition and French 75s. On September 3 he startled the country by announcing that the United States had traded 50 old destroyers for leases on British bases in the Caribbean. In addition the British made outright gifts of leases in Bermuda and Newfoundland. This deal, as Winston Churchill, now prime minister, later observed, was "a decidedly unneutral act," which by "all the standards of history" would have "justified the German Government in declaring war" upon the United States. But at a time when Hitler's undersea marauders were threatening Britain's control of her home waters, Roosevelt saw no alternative.

By this time Congress was completing a fierce debate over a bill for peacetime draft. Tempers ran so high that two Democratic House members exchanged punches. Senator Burton K. Wheeler of Montana warned: "Enact peacetime conscription and no longer will this be a free land." At one time mail to senators ran 90 per cent against the measure. However, polls taken at the same time showed most Americans strongly in favor. In mid-September 1940, Congress voted to conscript men between the ages of 21 and 35.

T HE presidential campaign of 1940 stepped up the debate over Roosevelt's policies. The dramatic events in Europe assured the President a nomination for a third term; he got it on the first ballot at the Democratic convention in July in Chicago. For a long time Roosevelt had been at odds with conservative Vice President Garner; now he dropped Garner and coerced the convention into choosing Henry Wallace, a former Republican with no following among Democratic machine leaders, as his running mate. (Afterward an indignant Louisiana delegate protested to George E. Allen: "No one wanted Wallace—absolutely no one. Name me just one man that did." Allen replied: "Brother, that I can do—and that one man was Roosevelt.")

The developments in Europe also shaped the Republican presidential nomination. No longer was it practicable to choose an isolationist like Senator Robert Taft of Ohio. The upheaval made possible one of the most dramatic events in U.S. political history: the meteoric rise of Wendell Willkie. An articulate utility magnate who had made something of a reputation as a foe of the TVA, Willkie was a lifelong Democrat who had voted for Roosevelt in 1932. But Willkie, a tousled, hoarse-voiced lawyer from Indiana, had a vivid personality which convinced influential Republicans that he would offer a real challenge to

Two cartoons comment on F.D.R.'s refusal to say whether he would run for a third term. Above, he coyly fishes in waters where the big one waits; below, his wife, writing her newspaper column, pleads: "But it would make such a nice scoop if you'd only tell me, Franklin." Roosevelt insisted he wanted to return to Hyde Park—but kept lining up convention delegates.

Isolationist Burton K. Wheeler rose to prominence as an ardent reformer. In his first term as senator he helped investigate President Harding's corrupt Attorney General, Harry Daugherty. Wheeler's early crusading became the basis of a 1939 hit motion picture, "Mr. Smith Goes to Washington."

Kansas' great editor, William Allen White of Emporia, backed many Roosevelt bills but always campaigned against F.D.R. During a 1936 campaign stop, the President spotted him in the crowd and said that he was grateful for "Bill White's support for three and a half years out of every four."

Roosevelt. Although as late as April 1940 Willkie still did not have one delegate committed to him, in June the Republican convention, stirred by the youthful Willkie supporters and manipulated by a group of party professionals led by Harold Stassen, nominated him on the sixth ballot.

Willkie announced that he was eager to take on "The Champ," but Roosevelt, playing his role of commander in chief to the hilt, ignored him. One Republican congressman protested: "Franklin Roosevelt is not running against Wendell Willkie. He's running against Adolf Hitler." In such a contest Willkie was at a decided disadvantage.

At the end of the summer Willkie was still seeking an issue. The third-term question, which many thought would be explosive, had little impact. Instead, Willkie came more and more to attack the President as a man who would lead the country into war. In a bitter speech in Baltimore, Willkie said of Roosevelt: "On the basis of his past performance with pledges to the people, you may expect we will be at war by April 1941 if he is elected." Yet at the end of the campaign, Willkie was asserting: "All of us—Republicans, Democrats, and Independents—believe in giving aid to the heroic British people."

In November Roosevelt was re-elected with 27 million votes to Willkie's 22 million. He had a wide margin in the Electoral College (449-82), although Willkie had cut his popular plurality to the smallest of any winner since 1916.

AFTER Election Day events abroad moved swiftly to bring war closer to America. On December 9 Roosevelt received an urgent message from Churchill. Britain was in "mortal danger"; it needed vast quantities of American arms; it was running out of cash. The President responded swiftly. On December 17 he unveiled a new proposal: to lend arms directly on the understanding that they would be returned or replaced when the war ended. "What I am trying to do," he said, "is to eliminate the dollar sign."

The "lend-lease" plan aroused intense opposition in Congress. "Lending war equipment is a good deal like lending chewing gum," Senator Taft protested. "You don't want it back." But the popular tide had turned. At election time, polls had revealed an even division of sentiment on whether to help Britain at the risk of war. By mid-January 1941, three months later, 68 per cent of those polled favored taking the risk. The Senate approved lend-lease by 60-31, the House by 317-71. By the end of March Congress had voted seven billion dollars as first installment on a huge program to arm the Allies.

All pretexts of neutrality had vanished. Moreover, it quickly came to seem illogical to spend great sums to produce munitions for the Allies, load them on ships and then take no steps to insure that the vessels got there safely. By April 1941 American naval vessels were patrolling far out into the Atlantic.

On May 27, 1941, the President proclaimed an unlimited national emergency. In June he froze German and Italian assets in America and closed their consulates. On June 22 Hitler brutally invaded his ally Russia.

On September 4 a Nazi U-boat attacked the United States destroyer *Greer* off Greenland. A week later, in a national radio broadcast, the President denounced German "piracy" and declared that he had ordered the Navy to shoot on sight these "rattlesnakes of the Atlantic." That fall Congress repealed restrictive sections of the Neutrality Act of 1939; henceforth the President could arm merchantmen and authorize ships to sail into combat areas.

While America worried about the danger of involvement in war in Europe, even more serious trouble was brewing with Japan. On September 27, 1940, the Japanese had entered into the Tripartite Pact with Germany and Italy, one section of which appeared to be aimed directly at the United States. Within the Administration, Ickes and Morgenthau urged the President to impose an economic embargo on Japan, especially on shipments of oil. But Hull and the President's defense advisers cautioned him against a policy which might precipitate a war for which the United States was unprepared. The militants won a partial triumph: Some items were embargoed, and the base of the Pacific Fleet was shifted from California to Pearl Harbor in Hawaii. But Roosevelt permitted most grades of oil to flow freely to Japan.

T HROUGH 1941 relations with Japan deteriorated rapidly. On July 25 Tokyo announced that it was establishing a joint protectorate over Indochina with Vichy France—the government of unoccupied southern France, which existed as a Nazi puppet state with Vichy as its capital. The Indochina move was a direct threat to the Philippines. The very next day President Roosevelt froze Japanese assets in the United States, in effect embargoing all trade with Japan, and with a stroke of the pen cutting the island empire off from the source of 80 per cent of its oil. Both sides began to prepare for war, though American military men urged caution and delay.

President Roosevelt wanted peace, but not at the price of major concessions to the Japanese. He took a strong line. The United States was demanding more of Japan than of any other power, insisting not merely that Tokyo abandon its plan for a drive to the south but that, after a costly war of more than four years, it withdraw from China.

Yet Japan had done much to invite distrust. It had presented to the world a spectacle of government by assassination, of military leaders who had often taken the initiative away from the heads of government. By the autumn of 1941 the Japanese militarists were impatient for war. The United States had telling evidence. A year before, a team of Army cryptanalysts had cracked Japan's major secret code, and America was privy to much of Tokyo's international military and diplomatic correspondence.

As early as January 1941 Ambassador Grew had warned: "There is a lot of talk around town to the effect that the Japanese, in case of a break with the United States, are planning to go all-out in a surprise mass attack on Pearl Harbor." But such an assault seemed unlikely; American naval experts were certain Japan lacked the necessary resources. In November 1941 observers spotted a Japanese expeditionary force south of Formosa, but they assumed it was headed toward Indochina, Malaya or the Indies.

On December 7, 1941, most of the country awoke to a beautiful sunny morning. The churches were crowded and the newspapers were filled with ads. The Matson Line was offering a vacation cruise to Hawaii. In Washington Cordell Hull went to his office in the State Department at 10:15 to await an answer to his latest—and last—proposals to Japan. At around noon he received a phone call: The Japanese envoys wished an appointment to deliver a reply. Five thousand miles to the west, in Hawaii, it was still early morning. At Hickam Field soldiers filed into the mess hall for breakfast; on the great battleships in the harbor, many sailors prepared for a day of rest; at Wheeler Field fliers still lay sleeping in their bunks—all of them unaware of the violence that was thundering toward them.

Henry Stimson, 72 when he was named Secretary of War, resented allegations that he was too old for the strenuous job. He summoned two young assistants, John J. McCloy and Robert Lovett, for a workout. Lovett recalled: "Next morning when I tried to get out of bed I fell over myself, I was that sore."

Frank Knox served Franklin Roosevelt well as Secretary of the Navy, but his favorite Roosevelt was Teddy, under whom he fought in the Spanish-American War and in the Bull Moose campaign of 1912. He adopted many of his idol's mannerisms, including a toothy grin and the exclamation "Bully!"

TEAMWORK is the theme of this sign stressing the partnership between the home-front worker and the men in uniform. This poster and those on the next pages were among thousands issued. One competition drew 2,000 entries, many by top artists.

Fighting the war on the home front

MONTHS before the attack on Pearl Harbor, the United States had already become "the arsenal of democracy," and the threat of war was rapidly turning it into "the home front." Men were drafted in peacetime, and government posters took on a martial tone (above). When war came it made profound changes in American life. Millions departed for the services. Millions more left their pleasant hometowns to live in drab rooms in hostile war-boom cities. The stream of women entering the labor force rose to a flood crest of almost 18 million. Well-fed Americans had their menus curtailed by food rationing. A people accustomed to going everywhere by car had to get used to gasoline rationing. A populace inured to waste was asked to save tin cans and rendered fats and to put up with citywide dim-outs to conserve power. Income taxes and living costs climbed—but many men were "frozen" in vital war jobs and could not take higher-paying work elsewhere.

Despite petty annoyances and profound upheavals, for most Americans on the home front the war years were a time of achievement as well as a time of anxiety. For during these years of total war, there was scarcely a man, woman or child who was not contributing to the national goal in some way. If there was concern over the war news, it was a concern that was shared with millions. Many Americans would recall the home-front years in a curious way as among the most purposeful—as well as the most tense—of their lives.

WOMAN WAR WORKERS join men in installing structural parts in a C-87 transport plane. Women proved to be capable, reliable factory hands, better than men at some tasks

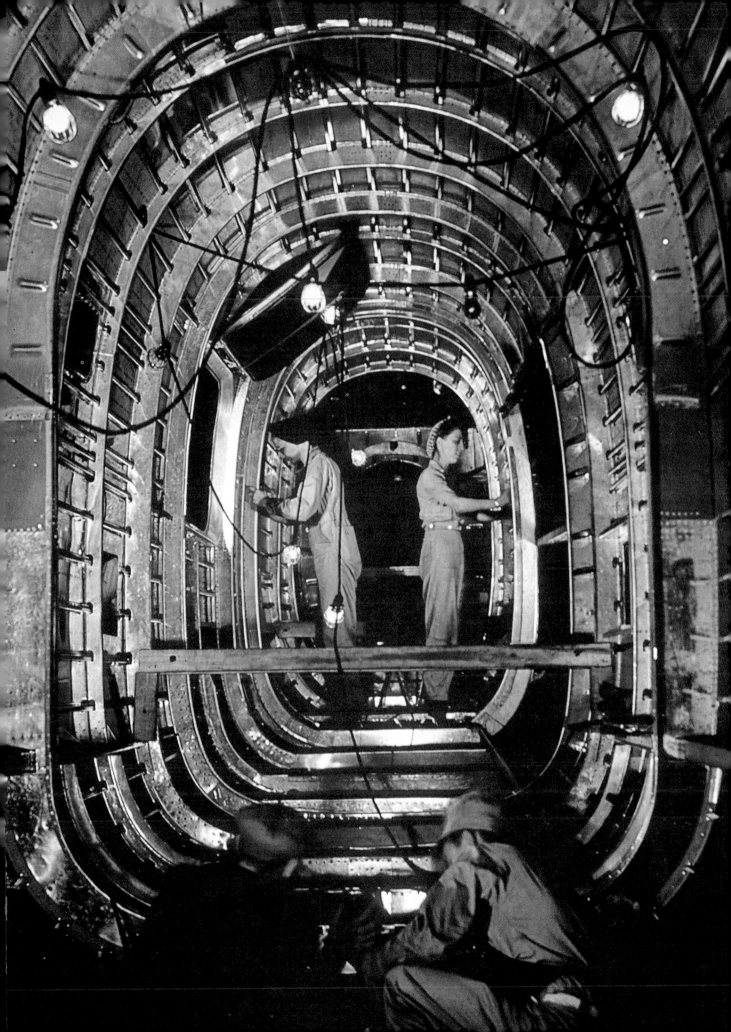

STANDING IN LINE, New Yorkers at a pork store attempt to stock up on smoked meats before rationing starts. After the last meat had been bought, police often had to disperse irate crowds left standing outside. Later, when an estimated 20 per cent of the total meat supply was moving through the black market, more than one butcher was assaulted by customers.

USE IT UP – WEAR IT OUT – MAKE IT DO!

OUR LABOR AND OUR GOODS ARE FIGHTING

Learning to live with less in a land of plenty

HOME-FRONT people worked much harder and longer, earned more money and had less to spend it on than ever before in their lives. So they bought war bonds, paid off old debts and had their teeth fixed. Men's trouser cuffs and the gay frills of women's clothes vanished along with unlimited steaks. Shoes were rationed and growing children used up many a family's ration points, leaving their parents to walk on thin soles. The list of scarcities and inconveniences was almost endless: coffee (some people tried adding a teaspoonful of new coffee to yesterday's grounds, with dubious results); cigarettes (some girls smoked cigars); liquor (to get a bottle of bourbon or rye a customer often had to buy a bottle of plentiful rum); train seats (many travelers had to stand up or perch on luggage in the aisles); plane seats (ticket holders with low-priority ratings were often "bumped" —left behind in favor of a government official or an industrial expert); reading matter (books were printed in smaller type, and some magazines were forced to limit circulation because of the paper shortage); hotel rooms (many travelers slept sitting up in lobby chairs). And to buy almost anything, Americans had to share that irksome new experience shown above—waiting in line.

WAITING FOR GASOLINE, motorists crowd around the single pump in operation at a Brooklyn service station. When gas shortages first became critical, a line of cars was often seen following tank trucks to the service stations. Gas rationing, begun on the East Coast in May 1942, was extended throughout the country that December primarily to conserve rubber.

USING LEG MAKEUP, girls caught by the wartime shortage of silk and nylon stockings paint their own. A few acrobatic women painted on seams too. European girls in the same fix usually settled for cotton or woolen stockings —or bare and unpainted legs.

A DIMMED-OUT DOME rises over the customarily floodlit Capitol building in Washington. The lights were turned off two days after Pearl Harbor as a precaution against air raids.

COLLECTING SCRAP METAL, New York children push a cartful of aluminum through Lower East Side streets in July 1941. The scrap drive was in full swing well before Pearl Harbor.

SCANNING THE SKY, an aircraft spotter in a post at Yarmouth, Maine, searches for enemy planes that never came. Her partner telephones a report to local air defense headquarters.

Doing something extra
to advance the war effort

THE people at home eagerly looked for useful things to do—and found them. They served on draft boards and rationing boards, flew private airplanes over coastal waters in search of U-boats, stood watch as aircraft spotters and, as air raid wardens, policed practice blackouts. Householders ran war-bond drives and took part in scrap-metal collections. They plowed vacant lots and planted enough "victory gardens" by 1944 to produce some 40 per cent of the fresh vegetables consumed at home. They gave 13 million pints of blood to be administered as plasma to the battle wounded.

The contributions of women were many and varied. As nurses' helpers they did chores in civilian and military hospitals. As Gray Ladies they visited hospitalized troops at home and abroad, dispensing cigarettes and often writing that first post-battle letter to a wounded man's family. As hostesses in USO canteens they danced with sailors back from war duty and with lonely soldiers in training camps far from home.

By mid-1943 the Office of Civilian Defense had some nine million volunteers, and four out of five people on the home front felt that they were doing something to help win the war. Many felt they were not doing enough.

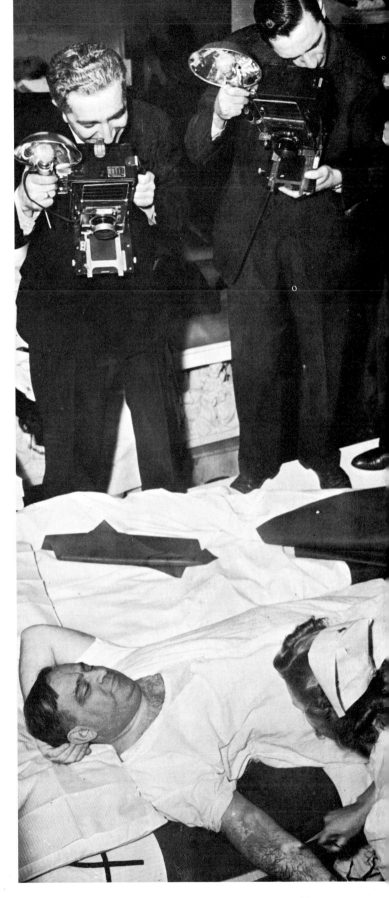

GIVING BLOOD, New York's Mayor Fiorello La Guardia publicizes the need for donations. At Pearl Harbor 970 men required emergency transfusions, with only 750 pints of blood on hand.

107

Plodding through the dust swirls of California's Owens Valley, Japanese-American évacués, torn from their homes, carry their luggage to

An injured Negro is jeered by whites as he sits waiting for an ambulance during Detroit rioting.

A ZOOT SUIT is worn by a Mexican youth *(above)* in dogged defiance of persecutors.

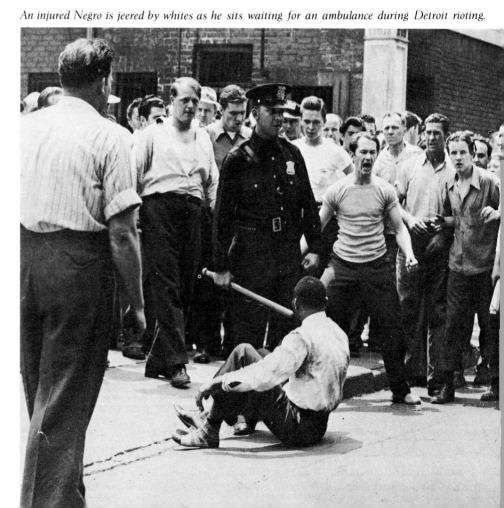

the tar-paper barracks that they would occupy from March 1942 until late in the war. Eventually this camp contained 10,000 internees.

Some ugly smirches
on the nation's war record

Most Americans went about their war work soberly, without the flag-waving hysteria that gripped the home front in World War I. Nevertheless, though posters proclaimed unity, there were ugly episodes of racial violence. In Detroit 34 men died as whites rioted against Negroes. In Los Angeles young Mexicans, usually attired in zoot suits, were persecuted by servicemen.

The harsh treatment of Japanese-Americans was in some ways most indefensible of all, because it resulted from government policy. The treachery of Japan's attack on Pearl Harbor, the savagery of the early fighting and the fears that mounted with each U.S. defeat—these combined to create panic in military and civilian leaders. More than 110,000 people of Japanese descent, two thirds of them American citizens, were taken from their homes on the West Coast and locked up in bleak concentration camps (above). Many stayed there for most of the war, though not a single act of sabotage or espionage was ever proved against them. The Japanese-Americans more than proved their loyalty with yeoman work as emergency farm hands and with gallant Army service in Italy. But it was not until 1944 that internees were permitted to return to the West Coast.

UNITED WE WIN

Hammering out the weapons to wage global war

FROM Henry J. Kaiser's Portland shipyards to Republic Aviation's fighter-plane plant on Long Island, America rang with the clamor of war production. As in World War I, the output of U.S. factories astonished the enemy, the Allies and even Americans themselves. The tempo of Southern industrialization was speeded. The production of steel and aluminum was vastly increased. A synthetic rubber industry was created almost out of nothing—and lifesaving drugs

Shipyard workers deck over a hull, last step before the launching that cleared the ways for a new keel. The ship, about half complete at

such as penicillin poured forth from the laboratories.

All this was done from a standing start. The German war machine which overran Europe in 1940 had taken eight years to build. That year U.S. arms production was negligible. Yet just two years later Americans were producing as much war material as Germany and Italy and Japan put together. In 1943 U.S. production was 50 per cent greater than that of the Axis; the next year it was more than twice as great. Though the U.S. armed forces absorbed 15 million men and women, civilian workers increased from 47 to 53 million. By the end of the war, the workers had produced 297,000 planes, 86,000 tanks, 6,500 naval vessels, 64,500 landing craft, 5,400 cargo ships, 315,000 artillery pieces, 4.2 million tons of artillery shells, 17 million rifles. Altogether, it was enough.

PACKING CARTRIDGE BELTS, women work in a Remington Arms factory. More than 41 billion bullets were produced in U.S. plants—about 1,400 rounds for every enemy in uniform.

launching, was finished up afloat. In 1942 freighters were being turned out in 80 days. By 1944 building time had been reduced to 22 days.

6. THE WAR FOR SURVIVAL

AT 1:50 p.m. on the sleepy Sunday afternoon of December 7, 1941, Chief Radioman Frank Ackerson in the Navy Department in Washington received an unbelievable dispatch from Honolulu: "AIR RAID, PEARL HARBOR —THIS IS NO DRILL." Three minutes before, a Japanese dive bomber, first of a wave of 183 carrier-based planes, had swept low over America's chief Pacific base. Flying to within 50 or 75 feet of the ground, the blazing suns clearly visible on their wings, dive bombers wreaked havoc on Wheeler, Hickam and other airfields. In a few minutes the Japanese virtually erased United States air power in Hawaii.

At the same time great formations of bombers came storming in over the American fleet tied up along Battleship Row. An armor-piercing bomb crashed through to the second deck of the battleship *Arizona* and triggered an explosion of hundreds of tons of powder. The *Arizona* gave a tremendous leap, then cracked in two as it settled to the bottom. The *West Virginia*, afire amidships, sank. The *Oklahoma*, struck by five torpedoes, rolled over in the shallow water and lay with her bottom pointing grotesquely toward the sky.

That afternoon, amidst the stench of burning oil, the roar of flames and the cries of the trapped and wounded, the Navy began to count its losses. The surprise raid had sunk or badly damaged 18 ships, destroyed 188 planes and damaged 159 more. More than 2,400 Americans were killed (nearly half in the explosion of the *Arizona*) and 1,178 were wounded. In two hours the Navy had

BANNERS FOR WAR are made by seamstresses in the Philadelphia Quartermaster Depot in 1942. Within a year the American flag was under fire from Burma to Bizerte.

lost about three times as many men as in the Spanish-American War and World War I combined. The damage might well have been worse. The Japanese had ignored Pearl Harbor's invaluable oil facilities, and Admiral William Halsey's carrier force chanced to be away on a special mission and hence escaped harm. Nonetheless the raid paralyzed the United States Pacific Fleet for many crucial weeks.

The news reached most Californians as they came home from church, Nebraskans as they sat down to Sunday dinner, New Yorkers when WOR interrupted its account of the Giant-Dodger football game from the Polo Grounds. Bewilderment turned to rage when Americans learned that at the very moment the Japanese were bombing Pearl Harbor, two envoys from Tokyo were carrying on the pretense of diplomatic negotiations with Secretary Hull.

The next day a grim President Roosevelt went before Congress. On December 7, he said, "a day which will live in infamy," the Japanese had launched an "unprovoked and dastardly attack" on American soil; he asked for a declaration of war. The Senate approved his request 82-0; the House 388-1; only Representative Jeannette Rankin of Montana, who had voted against the war resolution in 1917, cast a negative vote. Three days later Germany and Italy announced that they were at war with the United States.

During the war and afterward some of the President's foes would claim that a kind of diabolical conspiracy within the Administration had brought on the Pearl Harbor attack. There is no foundation for this view, but there is no question that the success of the attack reflected a lack of preparation on the part of the American government. Roosevelt's aides bungled the relay to Hawaii of intelligence decoded from Japanese messages, and both the government in Washington and the commanders in Hawaii were negligent in not taking proper precautions against a surprise raid.

But the Japanese committed the worst blunder. If they had chosen to penetrate Southeast Asia instead of attacking Hawaii, they might have won the resources they desired without provoking America to war.

The attack not only brought the United States into the fighting, but united the country as no other event could have. Americans everywhere responded to it with anger and determination.

The American reaction to Japan's attack on Pearl Harbor, reflected in the cartoon above, was shock and anger. Actually, the possibility of a sneak raid had not been overlooked. Eight months before, the Army and Navy air chiefs in Hawaii had suggested that carrier-based planes might attack at dawn from about 300 miles at sea —almost exactly what happened.

FEW Americans had any illusions about the kind of war it would be. Woodrow Wilson had called World War I a war to make the world "safe for democracy." Asked to describe World War II, Franklin Roosevelt responded that it was simply "the survival war." Under the levelheaded veteran newsman Elmer Davis, the Office of War Information offered an interpretation of the war which was far more restrained than that of the Creel Committee in World War I. In this war Americans did not rush into the streets waving flags and cheering the soldiers on to battle. There were no new martial songs like "Over There." In advertisements the immaculate soldier of the beginning of the war quickly gave way to the begrimed infantryman plodding through war-torn villages. The war reporters the country found most persuasive were those who, like columnist Ernie Pyle and cartoonist Bill Mauldin, showed their GIs unshaven, weary, bitter and profane. The country realized that the war would not end quickly or be fought easily. To dislodge Hitler from his control of the Continent would be a painful, bloody business. The road to Tokyo would be paved with the bodies of American men—some only now being hustled into training camps, some still at home with their wives and children, some mere boys in school.

Of the 31 million men who registered for the draft, nearly 10 million were inducted. Thirty-six per cent of registrants were put in the rejected class of 4-F, in part because doctors were now more skilled than in World War I at detecting mental instability. Hundreds of thousands more were turned down as illiterates. By war's end, some 15 million men and women had seen service: 10.4 million in the Army, 3.9 million in the Navy, 600,000 in the Marines and 242,000 in the Coast Guard. More than 200,000 women served in the armed forces as nurses or in the Women's Army Corps (WAC) or other auxiliaries.

The horrors of war touched the people at home only indirectly. On an outing in the Oregon mountains, some members of a fishing party were killed when a child picked up a Japanese bomb, one of several sent across the Pacific aboard paper balloons; but these were the only known casualties on American soil in World War II. American cities did not suffer the air raids which gutted Coventry, Rotterdam, Hamburg, Munich and Tokyo. In most cities in the United States, there were few visible signs of a nation at war. In the early months, "dim-outs" were imposed on East Coast cities to diminish the sky-glow which, by silhouetting Allied merchantmen at sea, betrayed them to Nazi U-boats. In late April 1942 Broadway's Great White Way was blacked out, and its lights did not go on again until May of 1945. But in most American cities, lights burned brightly at night through most of the war.

For the average American, the war was a dreary period of waiting. The war worker camped in a mean boom-town barracks felt a numbed sense of being deprived of much of his identity. The soldier's wife, living in a high-rent hovel near a training camp in order to be near her husband, found herself one of a nameless mass of "war wives," snatching at a few hours of pleasure before her husband received his orders to ship out. For many the war was a lonely time. For those with sons and husbands and fathers in the service, it was a long ordeal of anxiety and anguish, with millions of families constantly fearful of receiving a telegram beginning, "We regret to inform you. . . ."

In World War II firepower counted for more than derring-do; battles were usually won by the side which had massed the most planes, warships or artillery. Before the United States could hope to defeat the Axis, it had to turn itself into a mighty arsenal. With no little disorder and confusion, that is just what it did. When the Allies finally launched their invasion of Fortress Europe in 1944, the armies "lurched forward . . ." wrote historian Allan Nevins, "like a vast armed workshop; a congeries of factories on wheels with a bristling screen of troops and a cover of airplanes."

As early as the summer of 1940, a flood of "dollar-a-year men," most of them prominent businessmen, had moved into Washington to run the new mobilization. Fearful of placing dictatorial production powers in the hands of one man, Roosevelt worked at the start through various makeshift agencies, none of which proved effective. In January 1942 the President created the War Production Board under director Donald Nelson of Sears, Roebuck. Though Nelson was a first-rate technician, he was never able to impose effective control on priorities or work out a balanced system of production in which small business had a fair role. As late as the summer of 1942, innumerable bottlenecks were still impeding production.

In a 1941 cartoon, Japan pushes off on a risky course as its Axis partners watch. There was little teamwork or amity in the Axis, and Germany was caught completely by surprise by Pearl Harbor. Japan had no affection for the racist Nazis, while Hitler reputedly remarked after the fall of Singapore that he would gladly send 20 divisions to help repel the yellow man.

In October 1942, alarmed at the disorganization, Roosevelt named Supreme Court Justice James F. Byrnes to head a newly created Office of Economic Stabilization. Byrnes proved an excellent organizer. He immediately ended the confusion over priorities by establishing control over steel, aluminum and copper allocations. In May 1943 Byrnes turned the OES over to former Representative Fred Vinson of Kentucky in order to take on an even more powerful assignment as Director of the Office of War Mobilization. Byrnes, operating out of the White House, was dubbed "Assistant President." He antagonized labor and other interests by his rulings, and when he imposed a midnight curfew on bars and places of entertainment in 1945, many objected that the "Byrne-out" was motivated not by the desire to conserve coal and power but by the wish to police morals. But Byrnes had the confidence of his former colleagues in Congress, and he demonstrated that he could resolve the conflicting claims of generals and admirals, steel magnates and union leaders.

THE mobilization never did proceed with clockwork precision. But even in the confused year of 1941, production increased at an impressive pace. From 1939 to 1945, output nearly doubled. The defense and war drives built a magnesium industry, expanded the capacity for aluminum production almost nine times, increased electricity output to nearly half again as much as in 1937, enlarged machine-tool production sevenfold and turned out more iron and steel than the whole world had produced a few years before. By 1943 the output of American factories was far above that of all the Axis nations.

To meet the critical need for merchant shipping, the government turned to a master builder, Henry J. Kaiser. "The New Deal's Businessman," Kaiser had done most of his work for the government. As head of the outfit that built Boulder Dam, he had completed the job two years ahead of schedule. When he turned his talents to shipbuilding he set records that fixed the standard the Maritime Commission demanded of other firms. One of his ships was assembled in less than five days—complete with lifebelts, coat hangers and inkwells. Merchant-shipping construction, which had totaled only one million tons in 1941, exceeded 19 million just two years later.

The war speeded up the industrialization of the West by at least 20 years. By the middle of 1942 the three Pacific Coast states were building one third of the nation's ships, one fourth of its war planes. Soon they were producing huge quantities of rubber, aluminum and steel too.

Kaiser and other West Coast titans combed the country for workers. Many a Bronx boy who had never before left the New York area took a course in sheet-metal work and went to Seattle or Tacoma. In less than three years, San Diego's population doubled. Portland was filled to the bursting point; shipyard workers attended "swing-shift matinees" at movie houses from midnight to 4 a.m. Among those working for Douglas Aircraft at its six plants in California, Illinois and Oklahoma were orchestra conductor Werner Janssen, flyer Douglas "Wrong-Way" Corrigan, tennis champion Dorothy Bundy, dancer Ruth St. Denis, actress Betty Grable's sister, actress Carole Landis' mother, and a corps of midgets who were found invaluable for work in confined places.

The South, too, was shaken by the tremors of enormous migrations. The old Gulf seaport of Mobile with its elegant tree-shaded colonnades and mansard roofs had "slept for 230 years, then woke up in two." The population of Key West, Florida, leaped from 13,000 to 30,000 in two years. In 1940 there were only 90 shipyard workers in the state of Georgia; by mid-1943, Savannah alone employed more than 30,000.

The reshuffling of population during World War II comprised the greatest short-term migration in American history: More than 27 million people moved. People swarmed into defense towns where there were not enough schoolrooms for their children, not enough parks or playgrounds or hospitals or theaters or restaurants—above all, not enough dwellings to house them. In San Francisco people slept in refrigerator lockers, in automobiles, in tents and on the cement floors of garages. Landlords exploited a seller's market. An ad in Fort Worth specified: "Fur. Apt., no street walkers, home wreckers, drunks wanted; Couples must present marriage certificate." Ford's operation in Michigan typified the contrasts of wartime. The great bomber plant at Willow Run incorporated the most modern technological advances, but thousands of its employees lived, as one writer reported, "in squalid trailer camps, in pestilential shanty towns with privies in the back yard, or commuted 40 miles per day to and from their homes in Detroit."

Children raised in such mushroom cities found the war a time of bewildering disruptions. More than a million fathers were inducted, and many mothers went to work in offices and factories. Some of the "eight-hour orphans" were placed in child-care centers or nursery schools, which expanded greatly during the war. But more were "door-key children," who wore a key on a string around their necks so they could get into their empty homes when school let out. The uprooting of families occasioned a spectacular rise in juvenile delinquency. Court cases involving juveniles rose 56 per cent. Especially alarming was the rise of offenses by young girls.

A country which had spent 12 years trying to cope with an army of millions of unemployed suddenly found itself with an acute manpower shortage. Western Union "boys" were often elderly men. Millions of women went to work, most of them in the traditional white-collar fields, but many in the booming aircraft plants and shipyards. In ammunition plants, two out of every five workers were women. The number of women in the aircraft industry grew from 4,000 to 360,000. One woman worker in a munitions plant exclaimed: "I'm amazed at myself. I never could handle the simplest can openers, or drive a nail without getting hurt, and now I put in half my nights armed with hammers and wrenches handling the insides of giant machines."

THE war boom brought unprecedented prosperity to millions. Thanks largely to time-and-a-half payment for overtime work, weekly earnings in manufacturing rose 70 per cent. The Okies, the migratory farm workers who had been pariahs during the '30s, found themselves welcomed at employment offices. Domestics left the pantry for the assembly line. Men who had been jobless for years found themselves making $100 a week and better. Many seized on the war prosperity to buy their way out of debt. In 1944 a woman in a Kansas City bakery started a great row when she blurted out: "I hope the war lasts a long time so we can pay off our mortgage."

The net cash income of the American farmer soared more than 400 per cent from 1940 to 1945. The Department of Agriculture, which had been urging farmers to curb production, now turned its energies to persuading them to step up output. The transition was rough. In 1940, when hog prices were the lowest in six years, Secretary of Agriculture Claude Wickard stirred the anger

"Assistant President" James F. Byrnes was a masterful compromiser, but he could be tough. As wartime home-front czar, Byrnes tolerated no infringement on his authority. When Harry Hopkins, who lived in the White House, made a suggestion, Byrnes retorted, "Keep the hell out of my business."

Economic stabilizer Fred Vinson had been a congressman and a judge; after the war he became Treasury Secretary and Chief Justice. When a son of Vinson's considered following in his father's footsteps, Mrs. Vinson declared, "I hope he won't. I've had enough of government service in our family."

of the Corn Belt by urging an increase in production which conceivably might result in unsold surpluses that would drive prices still lower. Wickard later remembered the next year as a hard one—a time "when you were just betwixt and between, scared to death you wouldn't have enough, scared to death you'd have too much."

As personal income rose, the demand for civilian goods and services far exceeded the supply, and the country faced the danger of runaway inflation. Early in 1941 the President set up a price-control agency under the stumpy, cigar-smoking Leon Henderson, a man renowned more for his shrewdness as an economist than for his tact. Since Henderson had no real power, prices soared. By Pearl Harbor, prices of basic commodities were nearly 25 per cent higher than in September 1939. In January 1942 Congress heeded Roosevelt's plea for an Emergency Price Control Act which authorized the price administrator to place ceilings on prices and rents in certain areas and to subsidize producers in order to halt price rises.

T HE Office of Price Administration relied at first on piecemeal price-fixing. When this proved inadequate, the OPA imposed a General Maximum Price Regulation, which froze most prices and defense-area rents at their March 1942 levels. Henderson coupled "General Max" with a system of rationing which limited consumers to the amount of scarce goods they could buy with the coupons allotted them. Rationing was applied to automobiles, shoes, sugar, coffee and other scarce items. Weekend guests carried their red and blue stamps with them and presented them to the hostess. As the war went on, more and more items of food disappeared from the grocer's shelf. Yet despite rationing, most Americans ate better than they ever had before.

All kinds of items were in short supply. Men had to be content with cuffless trousers, and women were denied stockings made of nylon, the exciting new synthetic which had first appeared on the market in 1940. (The only nylon stockings manufactured legitimately were commissioned by the government as spy bait in Europe.) In 1944 cigarette shelves were usually bare and queues formed in the evening outside cigar stores to buy a limited ration. Because of travel restrictions, the professional baseball teams had to abandon spring training in the South. In 1944 the Boston Red Sox worked out in Medford, Massachusetts, the New York Yankees at Atlantic City.

In May 1942 U-boats were sinking oil tankers at such a rate that gasoline rationing had to be imposed on the Eastern Seaboard. No single restriction was taken with worse grace, for most Americans had long since forgotten how to move about without an automobile. To intensify the problem, Japan's conquest of the East Indies and Malaya cut the United States off from 90 per cent of its natural-rubber supply. Within a year tires were so scarce that they were not available even on the black market. Roosevelt named a committee headed by Bernard Baruch to seek a solution to the rubber shortage. The committee recommended that gasoline rationing, until then limited to the East, be made nationwide; it also proposed the imposition of a 35-mile-an-hour speed limit and the development of a vast new synthetic-rubber industry.

To build this industry the President named William Jeffers, president of the Union Pacific Railroad, as rubber czar. Jeffers operated so effectively that the United States turned out 762,000 tons of synthetic rubber in 1944—well above the normal annual consumption of natural rubber—and 820,000 tons

This WASP pilot, shown after ferrying a fighter plane, was one of 1,074 women fliers who took over noncombat aerial chores to free male pilots for fighting. Though successful, the WASP was deactivated after 27 months of service: By that time, there were enough male pilots available to do the job.

the next year. But gasoline rationing remained in effect throughout the country until the end of the war.

By the end of 1942 black markets flourished in every product that was in short supply. The cab driver who once guided his fares to a speakeasy now knew where gas coupons were sold. The bellboy turned his talents to procuring cartons of cigarettes. Perhaps the largest of the black markets was the one in meat. When a Chicago reporter wrote that the city's housewives were spending one million dollars a week on illegal meat, an enforcement officer scoffed that the estimate was too low.

The OPA under Henderson soon found itself deeply involved in controversy. People grumbled about high prices and shortages, about black markets and restrictions. The agency did not have enough agents to destroy the black market, and it lacked statutory authority to put a firm ceiling on prices. As food costs rose, unions stepped up pressure for commensurate wage increases. Vexed at congressional complacency toward the mounting inflation, the President sent a special message to Congress on September 7, 1942, demanding action by the first of October. Roosevelt added an extraordinary threat: "In the event that the Congress should fail to act, and act adequately, I shall accept the responsibility, and I will act." Congress thereupon authorized Roosevelt to stabilize prices and wages at their September 15 levels. The President also froze farm prices, extended rent control throughout the nation and forbade wage or salary rises without government approval.

In December 1942 foes of price control drove Henderson out of office and continued this campaign against his successor, former Michigan Senator Prentiss Brown. In April 1943 Roosevelt vetoed a new attempt by the farm bloc to circumvent controls and tried to quiet the restive labor unions. But when John L. Lewis defied the "hold-the-line" edict by calling a strike of his mine workers for May 1, the President seized the coal mines and virtually ordered the miners back to work. At the same time the OPA rolled back food prices; on June 1 meat, coffee and butter prices were cut 10 per cent.

The Administration had many skirmishes to fight thereafter, but the big battle had been won. In July Roosevelt replaced Brown with the talented advertising executive, Chester Bowles. Bowles achieved a small miracle in economic control. From the spring of 1943 until the end of the war, the cost of living rose less than 1.5 per cent.

Colonel Oveta Hobby, commander of the WACs, fought a long battle to improve conditions for her corps of women volunteers. WACs wore drab uniforms and lived in crude barracks with no provisions for privacy. Yet more than 100,000 served in the WAC, making it the largest of the women's services.

PRICE control was only one of a number of anti-inflationary devices. More popular was the campaign to persuade people that by investing in government bonds they were buying the guns and ammunition to equip their sons on the fighting fronts. (In fact, the guns would have been bought anyway; the purpose of war bonds was to soak up loose cash that created an inflationary pressure.) The country snapped up $100 billion in war bonds.

To curb inflation more directly, the government resorted to exceptionally heavy taxation. The Revenue Act of 1942, which President Roosevelt rightly called "the greatest tax bill in American history," was designed to raise the gigantic sum of seven billion dollars in additional revenue annually. It stepped up taxes on high incomes in several ways: an excess-profits tax of 90 per cent (10 per cent of which was refundable after the war); a corporate-income levy of up to 40 per cent; and sharply raised estate and gift taxes. The act also spread its net to catch people with low incomes. Under the new law 50

Mildred McAfee, Wellesley College president, was an object of campus pride when she became head of the WAVES. But she defied tradition when she escorted Madame Chiang Kai-shek, who was wearing slacks, around the campus. The startled faculty suddenly eased its opposition to slacks.

Colonel Benjamin Davis Jr. was one of the outstanding Negro soldiers of World War II. The fourth man of his race to be graduated from West Point, Davis commanded the 332nd Fighter Group, which destroyed well over 200 enemy planes in Southern Europe and won a Distinguished Unit Citation. In 1959 Davis became America's first Negro major general.

million people paid taxes, compared to 13 million in 1941. To make tax collection simpler and more palatable, the government in 1943 compelled employers to collect the taxes by payroll deductions. The pay-as-you-go plan, which was originated by Beardsley Ruml, treasurer of R. H. Macy & Company, made the "withholding tax" a household word for millions of Americans who had never paid a federal income tax before.

Congress later enacted an additional increase of $2.3 billion over Roosevelt's veto; he had asked for a staggering $16 billion. His stinging veto message prompted the angry resignation of Senate Majority Leader Alben Barkley. Roosevelt hastily soothed the senator with a friendly letter, and the Democrats re-elected Barkley majority leader. Although the President found the second tax boost disappointing, he had nonetheless achieved a considerable redistribution of income in wartime that had not been possible in the halcyon days of the New Deal. Wartime taxes hit the top 5 per cent of income receivers harder than at any time in the nation's history. And while net corporation income rose slightly during the war, in 1945 it was less than it had been in 1941.

Federal spending soared from nine billion dollars in 1940 to 95 billion in 1944; in mid-1943 the United States was spending at the rate of almost eight billion dollars a month. Total outlays in the four war years rose above $320 billion—twice the total of federal expenditure in all previous history. The national debt soared to $258 billion, almost six times what it was at Pearl Harbor. When in 1936 the New Deal spent eight billion dollars, critics had warned that Roosevelt was inviting national bankruptcy. But when government spending reached $98 billion in 1945, few were troubled; unemployment had disappeared, and the country was enjoying new levels cf prosperity and production. The war seemed to demonstrate the Keynesian hypothesis: With mounting public deficits, unemployment vanished.

New Deal policies were sustained in other ways during the war years. TVA, Grand Coulee and the other public power projects proved invaluable. Many of the social gains of the New Deal were strengthened and amplified. The War Labor Board safeguarded the collective-bargaining rights unions had won in the 1930s; union membership jumped to nearly 15 million by the war's end.

IN many aspects of American life, the war quickened the tempo of change (in college, students "accelerated"), but the changes wrought were not always for the better. As a farm agent reflected: "Looks like the war has speeded up every kind of process, good and bad, in this country."

The social ferment had an enormous impact on race relations. Many Negroes moved from the Deep South; wherever they went they met the special kinds of humiliation which told them that they were not accepted as Americans. When they gave their blood to the Red Cross, the blood was segregated. War plants cried for more help, but Negroes often found themselves turned away at the factory gate. In the Army they were segregated in barracks and mess halls; in addition most of them were assigned to menial labor. When white soldiers boarded troopships, the band played "God Bless America"; when Negroes marched up the plank, the band switched to "The Darktown Strutters' Ball."

But Negroes refused to submit passively to the denial of their rights. By 1944 the membership of the National Association for the Advancement of

Colored People had risen to 500,000, a 500 per cent increase since Pearl Harbor. Between 1940 and 1944 the number of Negroes employed as skilled craftsmen and foremen doubled.

The assertion of Negro rights inevitably accelerated racial tensions. In the first six months of 1943, more than three million man-hours were lost through strikes protesting the upgrading of Negroes. On a sultry Sunday night in June of that year, the worst race riot in a quarter of a century erupted in Detroit. Fighting spread all over the city; throughout the night, mobs roamed the streets of the grimy Negro slum, Paradise Valley. At daybreak black and white mobs stopped streetcars and hauled off workers on their way to work. The police displayed much more energy in checking Negro bands than white mobs, and public officials did nothing. Not until a middle-aged Negro had been shot by white youths ("Just for the hell of it," one of them said) was semimartial law proclaimed. Hundreds had been injured; 25 Negroes and nine whites were killed.

The Detroit riot was only one of a number of outbreaks. In Los Angeles a crowd of 3,000 beat and kicked a number of young Mexican-Americans. In Beaumont, Texas, white workers burned two blocks of Negro homes. A riot in Harlem did nearly a million dollars' worth of damage in a few hours. But these eruptions marked a turning point. Sobered by the display of race hatred, governors called for antidiscrimination statutes; citizens organized committees on race relations; attempts were made to bridge the gulf between the races.

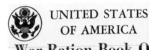

F OR all the humiliation and violence, World War II was a time of advance for the Negro. Since the Nazi doctrines of "blood" and "race" seemed embarrassingly similar to the credo of many American whites, the doctrine of white supremacy was subjected to a formidable intellectual assault. Negroes were slowly given a chance to prove themselves in the armed forces. Almost 8,000 were commissioned as officers. The all-Negro 99th Fighter Squadron won commendation in Europe and a combat team of the 93rd Infantry Division distinguished itself at Bougainville. Extremism began to diminish in the South. Georgia repealed its poll tax. In April 1944 the Supreme Court outlawed the white primary in Texas. Most important, race relations became what they had never been before: an indispensable cause of liberalism.

In most respects America's record on civil liberties in World War II compared highly favorably with that in World War I, largely because there was no significant opposition to the war and hence no grounds for organizing vigilantes to enforce conformity. The public's attitude toward conscientious objectors was considerably more tolerant than in World War I. The government jailed a few Nazi agents, clamped down on domestic fascists like the German-American Bund, and harried groups suspected of sympathy with the Axis. Father Coughlin's *Social Justice* was denied mailing privileges. But there was almost no vindictiveness against either German- or Italian-Americans and little evidence of spy hysteria.

To the generally exemplary record on civil liberties, there was one sorry exception: the relocation and internment of Japanese-Americans. In the weeks after Pearl Harbor, the West Coast, edgy over the possibility of a Japanese invasion, viewed with mounting alarm the 112,353 Japanese and Japanese-Americans (Nisei) who lived in the coastal states. The Hearst columnist Henry McLemore wrote: "Herd 'em up, pack 'em off and give 'em the inside

Most people obeyed rationing regulations; they used their ration books (above) when buying sugar and other commodities, and they bought only as much gasoline as their windshield stickers (below) allowed them ("A" stickers got a minimal supply). But there were crooks: One cache in Brooklyn had enough counterfeit ration stamps to last four million people a month.

Intransigent Sewell Avery was removed bodily from his office in Montgomery Ward for defying a wartime labor order, but he won out in the end. Twelve days later he was restored to his office. After eight months he lost control of the plant again. When the war was over, Washington finally gave up. One official admitted: "We haven't accomplished a damned thing."

room in the badlands." Even the distinguished journalist Walter Lippmann —long regarded as a defender of civil liberties—beat the drums for evacuation.

On February 19, 1942, President Roosevelt, bowing to the anti-Japanese hysteria, issued an executive order surrendering control to the Army, which ordered the removal of every "Japanese" (over two thirds were American citizens) from the West Coast. The Army commander on the West Coast, Lieutenant General John De Witt, proclaimed with stunning illogic: "The very fact that no sabotage has taken place to date is a disturbing and confirming indication that such action will be taken." Thousands were driven from their homes, to be dumped eventually into relocation camps in the Western deserts and the Arkansas swamplands. As disturbing as the action itself was the readiness of the Supreme Court to sanction it. In the Korematsu case, a divided Court set the perilous precedent that the rights of citizens in wartime could be set aside at the discretion of the President and military officers.

In a turnabout in 1944, the Army began wholesale recruiting of Nisei. The Nisei 442nd Regimental Combat Team became—for its size and length of service—the most decorated unit in United States military history. But for some white Americans, even this performance did not suffice. Toward the end of the war the Hood River, Oregon, post of the American Legion struck the names of 16 Japanese-American soldiers from their honor roll. There was a national protest. During the controversy one of the 16, Frank Hachiya, was killed on Leyte after volunteering for a dangerous scouting mission.

THE frictions of wartime made their mark on the politics of the period. The congressional elections of 1942 focused resentments over the conduct of the war. Like 1862, the year 1942 was a disheartening time of military setbacks and national indecisiveness. Women grieved over the drafting of 18-year-olds; farmers were unhappy about the order to put ceilings on crop prices; motorists griped about gas and tire rationing. In the elections the Republicans picked up nine seats in the Senate and 46 in the House, which they almost captured, plus 18 of the 32 governorships up for election. But these results were deceptive, for large numbers of war workers, who were predominantly Democrats, were on the move and had not met residence requirements in time to cast their ballots.

Though the meaning of the election was murky, conservatives interpreted the vote as a mandate for reaction. Power continued to gravitate toward a coalition of conservative Republicans and Southern Democrats. "Government by bureaucrats must be broken, and broken now," declared Representative Eugene Cox of Georgia.

In the first half of 1943 the coalition set out to dismantle the New Deal. Congress wiped out the National Youth Administration and destroyed the Farm Security Administration's program of aiding submarginal farmers. When the National Resources Planning Board recommended expansion of social security after the war, Congress abolished the board.

The congressional conservatives reflected the national exasperation with organized labor. Most of American labor adhered to a wartime "no-strike" pledge; the total loss in working time was only one ninth of 1 per cent, better than even the British record. But public attention focused on a few spectacular strikes. When John L. Lewis called a coal walkout in 1943, a furious Congress passed the Smith-Connally Act over a presidential veto. It authorized the President to seize strike-bound plants, compelled unions to "cool off" for 30 days and get the approval of their members by secret ballot before they could walk out, and prohibited unions from contributing directly to national political campaigns. Ostensibly a labor-reform law, the Smith-Connally Act was in fact a punitive piece of legislation. It failed to accomplish either its real or its stated purpose, but it did give labor a new weapon: official notice of a strike threat.

Although the President abandoned all emphasis on reform (for the duration, he said, "Dr. New Deal" must give way to "Dr. Win-the-War") both his powers and those of the federal bureaus increased. Since private interests were now expected to submit to the greater national interest, federal administrators were armed with new authority to discipline obstinate businessmen. The extent of this power was demonstrated during a strike at Montgomery Ward's Chicago plant in 1944. When Sewell Avery, the company's pugnacious and conservative board chairman, refused to settle with the union, the government seized the firm. Avery flatly refused to leave his office. Two husky, helmeted soldiers thereupon carried him out of the building.

I NSTEAD of terminating the struggle between liberals and conservatives, the war merely shifted the arena of combat. The question dividing the two groups now was how the war was to be conducted. To the liberals in Washington, Jesse Jones, head of the Reconstruction Finance Corporation, typified the administrator who pleased conservatives by attempting to procure scarce war materials with the methods of a profit-minded businessman instead of those of a mobilizer engaged in total war. Hero of the liberals was Vice President Henry Wallace, named by President Roosevelt to head a newly created Board of Economic Warfare. Wallace opposed Jones's "timid, business-as-usual procedure," and insisted on minimum labor standards in contracts which financed mining and rubber production in South America.

In June 1943 the Jones-Wallace dispute became a public brawl. Wallace charged that Jones had "failed dismally," and Jones said the Vice President was a liar and a squanderer. Embarrassed by the dispute, Roosevelt abolished the BEW and stripped the RFC of its foreign purchasing authority. Ostensibly an even-handed judgment, the President's action was in fact a victory for Jones, because Roosevelt created a new Office of Economic Warfare under Jones's ally, the conservative Leo Crowley, while the Vice President no longer had a major war function.

Wallace's quarrel with Jones had the ironic consequence of increasing his liberal support but destroying his public career. As the 1944 campaign neared, labor leaders led by Philip Murray and liberal senators led by Florida's Claude Pepper enthusiastically endorsed Wallace's claims for renomination. But organization Democrats, notably National Chairman Robert Hannegan, Mayor Ed Kelly of Chicago and the party's treasurer Ed Pauley, would not tolerate Wallace, in part because of ideological considerations, in part because they objected that Wallace was not "regular."

Roosevelt, wearied by his three terms in office and anxious to keep the party united, wanted to have Wallace as his running mate but he would not jeopardize party harmony. "I am just not going to go through a convention like 1940 again," the President stated. "It will split the party wide open, and it is already split enough."

The Office of Civilian Defense put millions of volunteers to work in dozens of jobs like the four represented by the emblems above: driver (top), messenger, rescue squad and air raid warden. A few activities produced amused reactions. When co-ordinators were appointed for paddle tennis and 62 other sports, one newspaper banteringly called for a co-ordinator of gin rummy.

Henry J. Kaiser, a prewar dam builder, became a mighty producer of war goods in World War II. His seven shipyards launched almost one fourth of America's entire wartime output of merchant shipping. He also started a steel mill and two magnesium plants, supplied cement for many fortifications and provided airplanes, artillery shells and aircraft parts.

He indicated he was willing to let Hannegan and his allies select a running mate for him, so long as their choice was acceptable to labor. Union leaders were now so powerful politically that they could exercise a veto on party decisions. In response to the small turnout in 1942, and the subsequent passage of the Smith-Connally Act, the CIO had organized a Political Action Committee in 1943 under the clothing union leader Sidney Hillman. When party leaders advanced the name of James F. Byrnes for the vice presidential spot, Roosevelt allegedly told them to "clear it with Sidney." Hillman turned down Byrnes as unacceptable to labor or Northern Negroes. When Bronx boss Ed Flynn also rejected Byrnes—because he had left the Roman Catholic fold for the Episcopal Church—Hannegan and his associates decided to look elsewhere.

The man they hit upon was Missouri's Senator Harry S. Truman. He was a logical choice. His management of the Senate committee investigating the defense program had won him a national reputation for courage and fair-dealing. As a "border-state Democrat," Truman stood at the intersection of the party's ideological axis. He was an internationalist on most issues, but he was personally close to isolationists like Burt Wheeler. He was a supporter of most New Deal legislation. Liberals and labor were impressed by his voting record, and party bosses were comforted by his personal loyalty to his sponsor, Kansas City boss Tom Pendergast. The New York *Times* called him "the new Missouri Compromise."

The third-term issue had caused some excitement in 1940, but the fourth-term question aroused little attention in 1944. By then, millions of Americans could not remember a time when there had been anyone in the White House but Roosevelt.

WHILE the Democrats had no trouble deciding on a presidential candidate, the matter proved more difficult for the Republicans. With each passing month, the gap between the views of Franklin Roosevelt and the 1940 G.O.P. candidate, Wendell Willkie, had narrowed. The former utility tycoon came to hold more and more liberal views on social questions and became an even more eloquent spokesman than the President on the need for an internationalist approach to foreign policy. In 1942 Willkie flew around the world. His account of the trip, *One World*, was a plea for international cooperation, and probably the most influential book published during the war. It sold more than two million copies, and both reflected and helped to create a remarkable shift of opinion away from traditional isolationism.

Yet isolationism had not disappeared. It had merely submerged. During the war it frequently took the guise of assaults on America's European allies. The isolationists adopted a "Japan-first" policy which reflected their deep distrust of commitments in Europe; their hero was General Douglas MacArthur, who, they claimed, was deliberately being denied the resources he needed to defeat the Japanese.

Willkie learned the strength of the Republican regulars when he rashly chose to battle for delegates to the 1944 G.O.P. convention in the isolationist stronghold of Wisconsin. He did not win one delegate; Governor Thomas E. Dewey of New York captured 15 delegates, while Harold Stassen won four and MacArthur three. Thereafter, the tight race for the Republican nomination became a runaway for Dewey, who was a proven vote getter in the populous

Northeast, young, vigorous and, like much of his party, middle-of-the-road.

In the campaign, however, Dewey operated under major handicaps. He could not find a real issue. His attacks on the Administration's mismanagement made little impact because the economy had been stabilized. Each time he criticized Roosevelt's handling of the war, newspapers reported a new Allied victory. His charge that the President was not giving enough support to MacArthur was offset by news of the general's triumphs in the Philippines.

Competent but colorless, Dewey at first waged a cautious campaign. Then, when he finally stepped up criticism of the President, he merely succeeded in stirring Roosevelt to make a devastating response. In a speech at a dinner of the Teamsters Union, Roosevelt commented on recent G.O.P. assaults on him, then said in mock indignation:

> "These Republican leaders have not been content with attacks on me, or my wife, or on my sons. No, not content with that, they now include my little dog, Fala. Well, of course, I don't resent attacks . . . but Fala *does* resent them. You know, Fala is Scotch, and being a Scottie, as soon as he learned that the Republican fiction writers, in Congress and out, had concocted a story that I had left him behind on the Aleutian Islands and had sent a destroyer back to find him—at a cost to the taxpayers of two or three, or eight or twenty million dollars—his Scotch soul was furious. He has not been the same dog since. I am accustomed to hearing malicious falsehoods about myself. . . . But I think I have a right to resent . . . libelous statements about my dog."

In the first wartime presidential election since 1864, Roosevelt won 432 electoral votes to his opponent's 99. The outstanding by-product was the rout of the isolationists. New internationalists like J. William Fulbright in Arkansas and Wayne Morse in Oregon strengthened the forces favoring world organization. After 24 years in the House, Representative Hamilton Fish, the leader of the isolationists in that chamber, was turned out of office. Taft narrowly escaped defeat in Ohio.

RETURNED to office by a comfortable margin and with a swollen majority in the House, Roosevelt began his fourth term with indications that Dr. Win-the-War would be retired from practice and Dr. New Deal summoned once again. In 1944 the President had outlined an economic bill of rights which included not only familiar New Deal items like the right to a remunerative job, but new emphases on health, education and social insurance. When Congress returned to Washington in January 1945, he showed the direction of his thinking by removing Jesse Jones as Secretary of Commerce and nominating Henry Wallace for his place, an act of very considerable symbolic importance.

New Deal liberals rejoiced that Roosevelt was once more assuming responsibility for a program of liberalism and internationalism. They looked forward to the postwar years as a time of new social gains and expanded world concourse. Some of these expectations were to be fulfilled. Yet there were in the politics of the war years the seeds of a different kind of postwar politics: the rebellion of Southern Democrats against the growing militance of the Negroes, the "martyrdom" of Henry Wallace, the desire to punish union leaders, the emphasis on "Asia first" and the apotheosis of Douglas MacArthur. America had yet to pay the price for the smoldering resentments the war had spawned.

War correspondent Ernie Pyle won great popularity among the GIs by sharing their risks in battle. He was once caught in a duel between a U.S. tank and a German pillbox. When Pyle returned, he explained apologetically that the tank crew had recognized him, "so I had to stop and talk." Pyle took one risk too many and was killed during the Okinawa campaign.

Conquering heroes, American soldiers in an amphibious vehicle receive a warm welcome from the citizens of a small Sicilian town in July 1943.

The assault on Hitler's fortress

THE Atlantic war was an attack on a fortified continent—Hitler's *Festung Europa*. From the United States' entry in the war in December 1941 to the moment of Germany's surrender in May 1945, this campaign hinged on one supreme effort: an allied invasion. All that went before was preparation: the tons of supplies, the vast air raids to soften up the fortress, the hard-fought campaigns to clear the Mediterranean front. The Normandy invasion that occurred June 6, 1944, was the mightiest feat of its kind in military history. Once it had succeeded, all that followed was inevitable, from the breakout *(opposite)* through the sweep to Paris and eastward, and the brief but bitter setbacks in the Low Countries, to the triumphant crossing of the Rhine and the surge through Germany to meet the westward-driving Russians.

Once the 3,000 submarine-infested miles of the Atlantic were behind, it was a compact war, fought primarily on—and above—a small, densely populated land mass *(see map, page 145)*. Thus it was a war of violent contrasts: of devastated towns on the one hand and liberated and joyous cities on the other; of children hiding from a rain of death one week and accepting handouts of American chewing gum the next; of tank columns knifing along poplar-lined highways and exhausted men a few miles away slogging up mountain trails—as the Allies relentlessly brought the war home to Hitler.

INFANTRYMEN ON THE MOVE escort a tank column through the ruins of Saint-Lô. The breakthrough here preceded by a 2,500-plane attack, opened the way to Paris.

A convoy of Allied freighters and tankers assembling for the perilous North Atlantic run is guarded by a protective screen of naval escorts,

A fight to the death against wolf packs of the sea

AMERICAN men and equipment flowed to Europe over a 3,000-mile supply line, under constant threat from submarines. To counter this menace, Allied shipping traveled in huge convoys guarded by swift, tough warships. Some of the deadliest fighting of the war occurred between these escorts and marauding U-boats.

The convoy shown on these pages sailed into a U-boat "wolf pack" one day in February 1943. Five times in the next 18 hours the cutter *Campbell* beat off submarine assaults. When a sixth attacker suddenly surfaced with its hull damaged, the *Campbell* raced to ram it. In the collision and gunfight that followed, the *Campbell*'s hull was ripped—but the sub sank. From the water a few survivors cried for help (one called out, "Hello, boys," his only English phrase), and the escort vessels pulled them aboard. On the *Campbell* all power failed as water flooded the engine room. All that night the vessel drifted, dark and silent—her skipper, wounded by flying shell fragments, on the bridge. Next day a Free Polish destroyer took off all but a skeleton crew. The rest rigged a patch over the hole and threw deck gear overboard to lighten the ship. For three tense days they lay in unseasonably calm seas, a helpless target for the first sub that spotted them. But all the heroism was not aboard the *Campbell*. On the fourth day a tug arrived, having made a daring unescorted voyage of 800 miles from the nearest port. It towed the *Campbell* to safety—to fight again in the endless battle of the Atlantic supply line.

CLOSING IN FOR THE KILL, the *Campbell* turns its spotlight and after guns on the sub it has just rammed. Beside the sub a direct hit from a 3-inch shell sends up a geyser.

including the Coast Guard cutter "Campbell" at left. Aboard the cutter was Anton Otto Fischer, who painted the scenes on these pages.

A P-51 MUSTANG is serviced at a base in England. By spring 1944 these long-range fighters, which could escort bombers on missions of up to 1,800 miles, reduced the bomber losses of the Eighth Air Force by fully 30 per cent.

A B-24 LIBERATOR, flying at chimney height, breaks through the smoke of burning oil refineries at Ploesti, Romania. This raid, 500 miles inside enemy territory in August 1943, cost 54 of the 177 bombers that took part.

Heavily laden B-17 Flying Fortresses take off from

A fierce and costly air campaign over German Europe

a field in England. Swarms of B-17s and B-24s based in Britain and Italy dropped almost a million tons of bombs on German-held territory.

IN 1942 American B-17s based in Britain staged their first bombing raid, on German-held Rouen. The U.S. favored precision daylight raids; the British, night saturation attacks. The American planes, clearly visible, were highly vulnerable. They flew in close formation, to bring massed firepower to bear on enemy fighters, and at high altitudes, to make small targets for German ground gunners. When possible they were escorted by friendly fighters. Nevertheless the German air force often turned American raids into furious aerial battles.

Although not all bomber attacks were effective—the Ploesti raid *(opposite)* did little lasting damage—experts later concluded that bombers had played a major role in defeating Germany. No one ever questioned the importance of fighters. Of the 30,700 German planes destroyed, U.S. fighters accounted for two thirds. The combat total taken by the Germans in return was 8,500 American fighters and 10,000 bombers—and 64,000 dead.

Slashing into the Continent's "soft underbelly"

FOR American ground forces, the war in the West began with the landings in North Africa in November 1942. Once the southern coast of the Mediterranean had been secured, the Allies decided to use Sicily as a steppingstone to Italy. But the "soft underbelly" of Europe proved agonizingly hard. Italy's plains were barricaded by winding rivers that had to be crossed repeatedly ("Every damned river in this country is named Volturno," complained one GI); the mountains were worse. Athwart the road to Rome stood the ancient Benedictine abbey of Monte Cassino. There in early 1944 the advance stalled in mud and rubble. In the end, men with rifles won where the machines of war proved useless.

IN TUNISIA raw American troops of the 34th division fight Germans among the stone walls and olive trees of Djebel Tahent, called Hill 609 for its height in meters. The Americans won the skirmish, shown in this painting by Fletcher Martin.

ON SICILY an American patrol *(left)* combs a smoking street of Messina for snipers left when the Germans retreated to the Italian mainland. The invasion of Sicily in July 1943 was the first major amphibious landing made on Italian soil.

IN ITALY Monte Cassino *(right)* rises above its ruined town. For four months the height was held by the Germans against artillery shelling, infantry attack and bomber raids.

On the eve of battle General Eisenhower gives a paratrooper a final word.

Jammed aboard a Navy landing craft, Army men make the

Their H-Hour at hand, U.S. troops wade toward Omaha Beach. German fire was deadly in this area, but by nightfall 34,250 Americans

A wounded man is helped from a raft after his landing craft sank.

Germans surrender at Utah Beach. Utah, the westernmost invasion

Channel voyage. During the night before D-Day many were seasick.

The triumph that was D-Day

OPERATION OVERLORD, the cross-Channel invasion of the Continent, got off a day late. Some 150,000 men, 1,500 tanks, 5,300 vessels and 12,000 planes had been assembled and the attack set for June 5. Then a storm, mightier than any force of man, roared in from the Atlantic. All had to be called off. The weathermen guessed things might ease by the 6th. The Supreme Commander, Dwight Eisenhower, listened, pondered and made his decision. "Well, we'll go," he said. They went, rushing in on the beaches in an amphibious assault of unprecedented magnitude. Allied casualties were 10,700—but as the day ended, the doom of the Axis had been sealed.

were ashore here, and 36,250 more had landed at Utah Beach.

beach, saw the first breakthrough, toward the port of Cherbourg.

A D-Day beach a few days later is a bustling military depot.

135

WEARY TANK CREWMEN warm themselves around a campfire (*left*) during a lull in the 1944-1945 winter fighting in the Vosges mountains. "The hardihood . . . of the Allied soldier," said General Eisenhower, was "never tested more thoroughly."

A SELF-PROPELLED GUN moves up (*right*) past another one in the ditch in the December 1944 battle of the Bulge. American soldiers in this campaign suffered as much from the weather as from the enemy. U.S. casualties in the Bulge were 77,000.

In a bitter winter, an agonizing setback

THE winter of 1944-1945 brought the German offensive known as the battle of the Bulge. The operation kicked off under clouds that grounded Allied air cover and helped the Wehrmacht drive a 60-mile wedge through thinly held American lines in the Ardennes Forest. In the confusion Germans in American uniforms infiltrated U.S. lines. Sentries countered by improvising passwords like "Who is Betty Grable's husband?" (The answer: trumpeter Harry James. Among those who did not know was General Omar Bradley, but he was allowed to pass anyway.) At last the drive was stopped. At surrounded Bastogne, General Anthony McAuliffe contemptuously refused to surrender. Men and tanks began to push the enemy back. Within a month "the greatest American battle of the war," as Churchill called it, was won. It marked the last organized German offensive.

As the Bulge begins to shrink, a lone U.S. tank advances along a road in the snowy Ardennes. By mid-January the Germans were in retreat.

EAST AND WEST MEET at a triumphant moment, as two officers, American and Russian, embrace to celebrate the linking of their units at the Elbe River in Germany.

A beaten foe and a moment of joy for the victors

The last great barrier to victory was the Rhine. On March 7, 1945, a platoon from the 9th Armored Division found the bridge at Remagen still standing—and seized it minutes before it was due to be blown up. In the next 10 days five divisions poured across this structure, fanning out to set up bridgeheads for still more troops. By the time the bridge collapsed (*right*) under Nazi air and artillery attacks, Germany was collapsing too. The Reich surrendered May 7. Americans and Russians, who had met at the Elbe, drank to each other in captured champagne. Far off in San Francisco, the United Nations was getting organized. Hitler was dead in a Berlin bunker, and his inhuman regime, which had terrorized Europe for a dozen years, was finally destroyed.

7. THE GRAND ALLIANCE

NEVER before had the United States fought a war like World War II. Americans battled in the jungles of Burma and the sands of the Sahara, in the frigid Aleutians and the torrid Solomons. American pilots swept the skies over Java and Libya, bombed Crete and the Dodecanese, dodged deadly flak over Tobruk and the Ruhr. American sailors and merchant seamen steamed past the fiords of the Vikings and the ancient ruins of Carthage; they died in the Indian Ocean, in the Baltic and within sight of Atlantic City.

For almost a century the United States had been fortune's child, enjoying the benefits of world power without having to meet the obligations of alliances and standing armies. The Americans of the 1940s paid part of the price. They died on foreign shores and distant seas, some 405,000 in all, including boys of 18 who were still on the threshold of life and men in their 30s who were just beginning to get on their feet after more than a decade of hard times.

For some who might otherwise have lived quiet, uneventful lives, the war brought excitement and glory. The United States had its share of martial heroes: Major Richard Bong, the nation's all-time air ace, who shot down 40 planes, 19 more than the great Eddie Rickenbacker had in World War I, only to die in a stateside crash; boyish Audie Murphy, the country's most decorated soldier; Sam Dealey, commander of the sub *Harder*, which sank four craft in five days but never returned from its sixth patrol; Dorie Miller, a Negro mess attendant who coolly fired a machine gun from the deck of the *West Virginia*

OLDERS OF HISTORY, Churchill, Roosevelt and Stalin
eet at Yalta to plan the final attacks on Germany and
pan and settle the disposition of captured territories.

as it burned at Pearl Harbor; a young PT-boat commander named John Fitzgerald Kennedy, whose vessel was shattered by a torpedo but who succeeded in saving his crew even though he himself was badly hurt.

But for many the war was mainly a time of monotony and routine. Some served on supply runs in the rear areas of the Pacific—traveling endlessly, like the crewmen in Thomas Heggen's book *Mr. Roberts*, "from Tedium to Apathy and back; about five days each way." Others spent long, tiresome hours standing watch on Coast Guard cutters, or endured the loneliness of the Arctic tundra, or were stranded at dreary communications posts on bleached coral islands, or were simply shunted from post to post in America.

Those in combat found war mostly a time of tension and fatigue. Their war, wrote correspondent Ernie Pyle, consisted "only of tired and dirty soldiers who are alive and don't want to die; of long darkened convoys in the middle of the night; of shocked silent men wandering back down the hill from battle; of chow lines and Atabrine tablets and foxholes and burning tanks and Arabs holding up eggs and the rustle of high-flown shells; of jeeps and petrol dumps and smelly bedding rolls and C rations . . . and of graves and graves and graves."

William F. "Bull" Halsey's first assignment, in 1904, was on the "Missouri." In 1945, as fleet commander, he anchored a new "Missouri" in Tokyo Bay. His tactics were to do the unexpected—fast. Halsey's rank rose until, he said, "one more stripe and I couldn't bend my arm to take a drink."

A FEW weeks after Pearl Harbor the United States signed a binding military alliance with the 25 other countries fighting the Axis. The members of the alliance—for which President Roosevelt coined the term "United Nations"—committed themselves to waging war to the fullest of their resources. Global strategy was co-ordinated with remarkable effectiveness, largely owing to the abiding trust and respect shared by Franklin Roosevelt and Winston Churchill. (At the end of one long cable to Churchill, Roosevelt wrote: "It is fun to be in the same decade with you.") British and other Allied military leaders worked closely with the American Joint Chiefs of Staff headed by Admiral William Leahy. For the Americans, General George C. Marshall and Admiral Ernest J. King directed military and naval operations.

Months before Pearl Harbor, American strategists had made one crucial decision: In the event of global war, first priority would be given to the European rather than the Pacific theater, for Hitler's Germany was considered the more formidable enemy. Even so, time would be needed before the full might of America could be brought to bear in Europe. Until then American troops could do little more than help to push back the outposts of Hitler's empire.

In October 1942 the first step in this process was taken when a United States naval task force departed Hampton Roads, Virginia, bound for the African coast. There it joined another huge expeditionary force headed south from England, where American soldiers had been stationed for many weeks. Commanding the North African invasion was a little-known American general, Dwight David Eisenhower, who had won a good reputation among military men during field maneuvers in Louisiana in 1941.

After Pearl Harbor, Commander in Chief of the Pacific Fleet Chester Nimitz had a battered fleet and an enormous area of command— 64 million square miles. Nimitz saw his task fighting the Japanese as "simple arithmetic—subtraction for them and addition for us." His total: a huge, victorious fleet.

On November 8 the Anglo-American forces landed in North Africa. A few days before at El Alamein in Egypt, Field Marshal Bernard Law Montgomery's British Commonwealth troops, strengthened by the arrival of 400 U.S. Sherman tanks, had sent the Nazi legions of General Erwin Rommel reeling in retreat across the Libyan desert. The American forces, still green, were battered by Rommel at Kasserine Pass in February of 1943. But they were learning. They had to go into action by dark, shivering in the unexpectedly cold African nights, stumbling across rough, mine-strewn terrain. But that spring they outfought the Germans in Tunisia. As Eisenhower's army drove eastward and Montgomery's forces thrust westward, the Germans were caught in the jaws of an enormous vise. On May 7 Bizerte and Tunis fell to Americans of General Omar Bradley's corps, and the fighting in Africa was all but ended.

The European war had reached a turning point. In the East, the Russians had turned back Hitler's armies at Stalingrad and mounted a vast offensive. In the West, the Allies had reopened the Mediterranean and exposed Southern Europe to invasion. Churchill later wrote: "It may almost be said, 'Before Alamein we never had a victory. After Alamein we never had a defeat.'"

The next British-American operation had already been decided. Joseph Stalin had been demanding a "second front" in Europe to pull German units away from the Russian front. Churchill, reluctant to launch a costly attack across the English Channel without some assurance of success, insisted on a circuitous approach, beginning with invasion of Sicily and Italy. Roosevelt agreed.

On July 10, 1943, some 160,000 Allied troops launched their first amphibious attack on Axis territory, coming ashore on the beaches of Sicily. The British Eighth Army under Montgomery and the United States Seventh Army under General George Patton swept across the island; in five weeks the fighting was over and the armies were ready for the next step.

As the Allies crossed from Sicily to Italy in September, news that the Italian government had surrendered gave promise of easy landings. But on Italy's beaches they found not disorganized Italians but resolute Germans. Nevertheless, the Allies quickly cleared out southern Italy, and by October 1 the American Fifth Army under Lieutenant General Mark Clark had entered Naples.

Here the advance slowed. For the next year and a half the Allies fought a bitter, dreary war. Nothing went right. The Germans had all the advantages of the terrain, and the Americans and British were outgeneraled by Field Marshal Albert Kesselring. In January 1944 the Allies attempted to outflank Kesselring by landing behind German lines at Anzio, 37 miles south of Rome. But the Germans pounced on the Allied beachhead, and mercilessly shelled the besieged invaders. It was not until June 4, 1944, that Clark's weary forces trailed into Rome, and many months of brutal campaigning still lay ahead.

WHILE Allied soldiers pressed their attacks on what Winston Churchill had mistakenly called "the soft underbelly" of Europe, Allied strategists stepped up preparations for the great attack across the English Channel.

To insure a successful invasion, certain preliminary objectives had to be achieved. In 1942 the Germans were winning the Battle of the Atlantic. That year over eight million tons of Allied and neutral shipping was destroyed by enemy ships, planes and mines. On the fearful run to Murmansk and Archangel, nearly one fourth of all ships carrying lend-lease goods to Russia were sunk.

In early 1943 the Battle of the Atlantic reached a turning point. March saw terrible losses, but by that spring Admiral King had developed an extensive program to cope with the U-boat menace. The convoy system was improved, and hundreds of escorts were added. British and American scientists made notable contributions. "Radio Detecting and Ranging"—also known as radar —was a British development that located distant or hidden objects by radio waves. Together with sonar, an underwater sound detection apparatus developed in the United States, radar proved invaluable as a submarine spotter.

Monthly losses were halved between March and May 1943; the number of

General George S. Patton Jr., who believed battle was "the most magnificent competition in which a human being can indulge," battled the Germans back through North Africa, Sicily, France and, ultimately, Germany. "It makes no difference what part of Europe you kill Germans in," said Patton.

Germany's air force met a tough rival in General Carl Spaatz's Eighth Air Force. After directing the American air attack in North Africa and Italy, Spaatz supervised the bombing of Germany. "What's the use of bombing rabbits in Italy," he asked, "when you can bomb wildcats in Germany?"

143

U-boats destroyed in these months mounted from 15 to 38. During the summer of 1944, when the vital Battle of France was being waged, not one Allied vessel was torpedoed in the North Atlantic. For the first time in the war the Allies had seized firm command of the seas.

No less important to a successful invasion was supremacy in the air. While the British undertook mass night bombings of German industrial targets, the more heavily armored American Flying Fortresses and Liberators engaged in so-called pin-point daylight bombing. But daylight bombing was more dangerous; six days in October 1943, culminating with a disastrous sortie on Schweinfurt, cost the Air Force 148 bombers and hundreds of men, mostly to fighter attack. The price was too great; American commanders halted daylight raids until long-range fighter planes arrived in substantial numbers early in 1944. In February the daylight raids resumed. By the spring of 1944 Germany's transportation system was on the verge of collapse, and the Luftwaffe had been swept from the skies. On D-Day Eisenhower was able to tell his troops: "If you see fighting aircraft over you, they will be ours."

Eisenhower had arrived in London in January 1944 to take charge of Operation Overlord, the long-awaited invasion of France. By the first week in June all was ready, with "the mighty host," as Eisenhower later wrote, "tense as a coiled spring . . . coiled for the moment when its energy should be released and it would vault the English Channel in the greatest amphibious assault ever attempted."

Shortly after midnight on June 6, three airborne divisions were dropped behind German lines. Each paratrooper carried about $10 worth of newly minted French currency, a small United States flag sewn on his right sleeve and a dime-store metal cricket to signal with at night. Out they tumbled, some right on target in Normandy, some scattered miles from their objectives, some to drown in flooded lands or in the sea.

As daybreak neared, the great armada approached France. After an intense sea and air bombardment, the heavily laden troops, cold, wet and seasick, clambered down cargo nets to the small craft bobbing in the heavy seas. At 6:30 they hit the beach at five points. Most resistance was light, for the Germans had been decoyed by clever British stratagems into concentrating their defense elsewhere. But at Omaha Beach, one of Rommel's crack units chanced to be maneuvering. For the invaders everything seemed to go wrong. Cloud cover had made aerial bombing ineffective; artillery sank at sea; the engineers were unable to blast the treacherous underwater obstacles. The German guns, emplaced on high bluffs above the beach, laid down a murderous fire.

But gradually the Americans scaled the bluffs. Mile by mile, they fought their way inland. Within two weeks British, American and Canadian soldiers had established a bridgehead along 60 miles of the coast.

BEFORE the invasion, Churchill had told Eisenhower: "Liberate Paris by Christmas and none of us can ask for more." On July 25 the invaders burst out of their bridgehead and raced toward the French capital. It was August 25 when Free French forces rode through the boulevards of the liberated city to the cheers of joyous Parisians. Ten days before, the American Seventh Army under Lieutenant General Alexander Patch had invaded southern France. Patch's army plunged north along the Rhone; by mid-September it had joined with General George Patton's force, speeding southward from Normandy. By

ALLIED INVADERS
ON THE ROAD TO ROME

This map and the one opposite show the routes (arrows) and key objectives (with date of capture) taken in Allied assaults on Hitler's empire. In May 1943 Allied units in North Africa converged to seize major Tunisian ports. From these and other bases, amphibious and airborne troops overran Sicily in five weeks. After several landings in southern Italy, Allied armies raced up the peninsula. North of Naples, German resistance stiffened, imperiling an advance landing at Anzio. But by early June 1944 the Allies had reached positions north of Rome (dotted line).

November the rapid Allied advance had cleared all Germans out of France.

That fall there was actually some hope that the war might be ended by Christmas. In October the Americans pierced the Siegfried Line, and the route into Germany seemed open. But Hitler had one final surprise in store.

On December 16, 1944, some 250,000 Germans launched a savage counter-offensive in the Ardennes Forest, aiming to split the Allied lines in a drive all the way to the sea. Screened by a thick fog and striking along a 75-mile front, they caught the United States First Army completely by surprise. A vast, chaotic battle raged. As the Panzer onslaught drove forward some 60 miles, maps of the Western Front showed a marked bulge in the Allied line. The American 101st Airborne Division was rushed up from France to hold the vital Belgian crossroads town of Bastogne. Eight German armored and infantry divisions surrounded the soldiers of the 101st. On the third day of a bristling siege, the Germans presented an ultimatum: surrender or face annihilation. General Anthony McAuliffe sent back a classic one-word response: "Nuts!"

The day after Christmas, one of Patton's armored divisions drove into the bulge from the south and broke the siege of Bastogne. From the north First Army units drove to meet Patton. By late January the bulge had been wiped out. The German offensive had cost the United States 77,000 casualties—but it had cost the Germans 120,000 and had drained them of the capacity to put up an effective defense. No longer could an Allied victory in Europe be denied.

THE war in the Pacific followed the same pattern as that in Europe: early defeat, a holding action, then an irresistible Allied advance. But in the days after Pearl Harbor, there was no glimmer of hope in the news from the Pacific. Although General Douglas MacArthur's command had been notified of the Pearl Harbor assault, Japanese pilots flying over Manila's Clark Field nine hours later found row upon row of Flying Fortresses and P-40s parked in the sun almost unprotected. In a single raid the Japanese wiped out half of MacArthur's total bombing force and a large percentage of his fighters.

Disasters mounted. Guam fell on December 11, 1941; Wake Island on December 23; Hong Kong on Christmas Day; "impregnable" Singapore on February 15. Japanese forces conquered the East Indies, overran most of Burma, moved into New Britain and the Solomons, and won control of the Indian Ocean and the Bay of Bengal. Five months after Pearl Harbor the Japanese held an empire extending south almost to Australia and west to British India. No conquest in modern history had been so quick or so far-reaching.

In the Philippines MacArthur fought vainly to stem the tide. He abandoned Manila and withdrew to the Bataan peninsula for a desperate last stand. But medical supplies ran out, and food became so scarce that the Army was fed mule meat. When it was clear that the end was not far off, President Roosevelt ordered MacArthur to leave the islands and take command of United Nations forces in Australia. The general departed, vowing to return.

On April 9 Filipino and American forces on Bataan capitulated. In the weeks that followed, more than 78,000 captives were forced on an inhuman 85-mile "death march" to Japanese prison camps. Thousands of them died. MacArthur's successor, General Jonathan Wainwright, retreated meanwhile to the island fortress of Corregidor with the remnants of his army. A month after the fall of Bataan, Wainwright too was compelled to surrender. On May 6, 1942, the last American flag in the Far East was run down.

CARRYING THE WAR
INTO HITLER'S GERMANY

Two days after taking Rome, the Allies began invading Normandy (1). Bursting out of the beachhead, some U.S. units rolled into Paris, while the Third Army met the Seventh Army, which had landed near Toulon (2). The Germans, driven out of France, launched a counteroffensive which briefly isolated Bastogne in December 1944. Striking through Germany, the U.S. Seventh Army linked up at Brenner Pass (3) with the Fifth Army, the First Army met the Russians at Torgau (4), and the Third Army halted near the Russians in Austria (5) at war's end.

Generalissimo Chiang Kai-shek had struggled for years to unite China when Japan attacked in 1937. "If China ventures to fight the Japanese," Chiang prophesied, "the Communists will attack from the rear and chaos will quickly overtake the country." China did fight, and after Japan's defeat, the Chinese Reds did attack from the rear, and Communism seized power.

That marked the low point of Allied fortunes in the Pacific. In the months that followed, American and British forces slowly stemmed the Japanese tide; at last worried Americans at home began to receive better news. In May a Japanese armada struck south through the Coral Sea, headed toward Port Moresby, New Guinea. An American fleet cut the Japanese off, and carrier-borne planes turned the attackers back. For the first time in history, a battle was fought in which battleships exchanged no shots and never saw each other.

A month later, at the battle of Midway, Admiral Chester Nimitz outfoxed a Japanese fleet trying to capture Midway Island and neutralize Hawaii. In one of the decisive naval battles of the war, the Americans, once again outnumbered, sank four of the best Japanese carriers and their air complements. But of 41 U.S. torpedo planes, only six returned to their carriers. That night in the carrier *Hornet's* ward room, one writer noted: "The empty chairs stood there in silent question and even on a night of victory voices were hushed."

But the Japanese had been halted. Now it was the Allies' turn. In midsummer of 1942 the United States began a limited offensive in New Guinea and the Solomon Islands. The fighting was fierce. Marines landing in the Solomons faced murderous machine gun fire; the water literally ran red with their blood. Once ashore they waded through deep swamps in mud up to their armpits, slept in water-filled foxholes, flushed the Japanese out of dense grass, out of limestone caves, out of concrete pillboxes. They learned to adapt themselves to a barbaric warfare in which no quarter was given by either side. The worst of jungle fighting was the strain of battling an unseen enemy. A Marine would fall, the victim of a hidden sniper. Enemy soldiers would appear suddenly and rush forward screaming, "Marine, you die!" The Japanese would infiltrate by night and induce Americans to expose themselves by whispering from the jungle: "Marine, I'm a Marine. Wounded. Joe, Joe, where are you?"

After a half year of vicious combat in the steaming jungles of the Solomons, the Americans wrested the island of Guadalcanal from the Japanese. American and Australian forces cleared New Guinea in furious fighting that cost them almost 90 per cent of their men dead, wounded or ill. At sea six major battles were fought in four months; the water around Savo Island, strewn with hulls of sunken vessels, was renamed Ironbottom Sound. When the fighting was over the United States held control of the seas. After Guadalcanal the United States Navy never lost another battle to the Japanese.

With naval support, Allied troops began to close in on Japan. In the Central Pacific, Americans under Admiral Nimitz launched a series of "stepping stone" assaults. At "Bloody Tarawa" in the Gilberts they met fierce resistance; the enemy had to be dug out, blasted out and burned out. But by August 1944 the United States forces had cracked the outer rim of Japanese defenses and captured key islands in the Marianas, only 1,350 miles from Tokyo.

WHILE Nimitz was clearing out the Central Pacific, MacArthur and the pugnacious Admiral William "Bull" Halsey were leapfrogging through the southern seas. They bypassed Japanese strong points and assaulted less well-fortified places that could serve as springboards to the Philippines. On October 20 MacArthur fulfilled his pledge to the Filipinos of 30 months before. Splashing ashore at Leyte, he issued a declaration. "People of the Philippines," he announced, "I have returned."

That week the Japanese made one last frantic attempt to hold on to the archipelago. On October 24, 25 and 26, they sent out three separate naval-air armadas. When Commander David McClintock of the sub *Darter* checked his last radar bearing through his periscope he gasped in astonishment. Ahead lay two parallel columns of enemy battleships and cruisers, flanked by destroyers. "My God!" exclaimed his aide. "It must be the whole Jap Fleet!"

In the battle for Leyte Gulf that followed, Japan risked everything—and lost. When the shooting was over, almost its entire fleet had been destroyed: three battleships, four carriers, nine cruisers, eight destroyers. Now there was nothing standing in the way of further landings. At the end of January 1945 some 100,000 Americans waded ashore on Luzon. In February, after fierce house-to-house fighting, the war-torn capital of Manila was freed.

While the reconquest of the Philippines was being completed, the Allies were carrying out a war of attrition aimed at Japan itself. American submarines swept the Pacific of more than half of Japan's merchant fleet; the home islands were cut off from crucial supplies of food and raw materials. Even more devastating was the accelerated air attack by the new B-29 Superfortresses based in the Marianas. The B-29 raid on March 9 and 10 burned to death some 84,000 in Tokyo. Fire raids burned out Yokohama, Osaka and other leading cities. Slowly Japan was being pounded into submission.

As victory neared in both the Pacific and European theaters, the Allied leaders gave increasing attention to shaping the postwar world. Even before the United States entered the war, President Roosevelt had been concerned with formulating postwar aims. In January 1941 he had enunciated the Four Freedoms: freedom of speech and worship, freedom from fear and want. That summer, in the foggy Atlantic off Newfoundland, the President met Prime Minister Churchill on a British battleship. The two leaders drew up an eight-point declaration known as the Atlantic Charter. It denounced territorial aggrandizement or changes of boundaries against the wishes of the people concerned; it spoke out for free access to trade and raw materials.

Once the United States entered the war, Roosevelt found that the global conflict required global diplomacy. In January 1943 he disappeared from Washington; a few days later he turned up in North Africa. Never before had an American President left the nation in wartime; none since Lincoln had visited a war zone. At Casablanca Roosevelt conferred with Churchill on both political and military strategy. The President was determined not to repeat the mistakes of World War I, when the Allies had framed terms of peace which later permitted Hitler to argue that Germany had been not defeated in war, but betrayed by its government. At a joint press conference with Churchill on January 24, the President announced the peace terms the Allies would offer the Axis: "unconditional surrender." Critics would later argue that this was a great mistake, claiming that it stiffened German will to resist. In fact, it is questionable whether it had much influence on subsequent developments.

Roosevelt was already beginning to discover that war had its own way of shaping the peace. When Allied troops landed in North Africa, they had encountered heavy resistance from forces of Vichy France; to cut down Allied losses, Eisenhower had negotiated an armistice with the French. Later he signed an armistice with an Italian government headed by Marshal Pietro Badoglio, famed as the commander of the brutal 1935 invasion of Ethiopia. Although Roosevelt explained these arrangements on the grounds that they

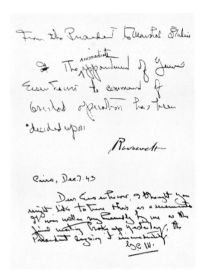

This note, signed by Roosevelt and hastily scribbled by General Marshall, informed Stalin of the appointment of General Dwight D. Eisenhower as commander of Operation Overlord, the invasion of Normandy. Eisenhower's rise to top command had been swift. In 1939 he was so little known that one press photograph called him "Lt. Col. D. D. Ersenbeing."

saved thousands of lives, some Americans were dismayed at the idea that expediency rather than idealism would redraw the political map of Europe.

The truth is that Roosevelt often followed the expedient course to some idealistic goal. He did not waver, for example, in his determination to create a postwar international organization with authority to preserve the peace. At Quebec in August 1943, Secretary of State Hull and Foreign Secretary Eden approved the draft of a Four Power Declaration which pledged America and Britain to work with the U.S.S.R. and China to create an effective postwar world organization. In October at Moscow the Russians agreed to the Four Power Declaration, approved an American plan for the postwar treatment of Germany and reached accords on Austria and the punishment of war crimes.

Cartoon soldiers like Bill Mauldin's Willie and Joe did much to deflate the notion of glamorous war. Here Willie, about to get a medal, says, "Just gimme a couple aspirin. I already got a Purple Heart." Mauldin helped civilians understand "these strange, mud-caked creatures who fight the war."

THE success of the Moscow conferences heightened America's good feeling toward Soviet Russia. Originally suspicious of their ally, Americans had come to admire the Russians and their courageous resistance to the Nazis. Yet there was still some uneasiness about Soviet attitudes. Especially troublesome was the question of Poland: Stalin seemed determined to deal with a Polish government only if it was one he could manipulate. To resolve this and other problems, and to cement the alliance of the great powers, on November 13, 1943, Roosevelt set out again on an arduous journey across the Atlantic. First the President conferred at Cairo with Churchill and Chiang Kai-shek. The three leaders agreed to restore Manchuria, Formosa and the Pescadores to China, to guarantee the independence of Korea, and to confine Japan to her home islands after the war.

From Cairo Roosevelt and Churchill flew to Teheran to meet Stalin. In four days of discussion, the three leaders thrashed out plans for the cross-Channel invasion and for a postwar United Nations organization. They also reached a decision on Poland, one that disregarded the principles of the Atlantic Charter: parts of eastern Poland would go to Russia, Poland would be compensated by a chunk of Germany.

Teheran represented the high point of good will among the Big Three. When Roosevelt returned to the United States he gave a Christmas Eve fireside chat in which he called Stalin "a man who combines a tremendous, relentless determination with a stalwart good humor. I believe he is truly representative of the heart and soul of Russia; and I believe that we are going to get along very well with him and the Russian people—very well indeed."

But by early 1945, with victory in sight, policy disagreements again threatened the unity of the Big Three. Once more Roosevelt, Churchill and Stalin met, this time at Yalta in the Crimea. From February 4 to 11, 1945, the three leaders drew the map of the postwar world. Disputes over the formation of the United Nations organization were settled amicably; the Russians accepted arrangements which—at this time, at least—seemed to virtually assure Anglo-American control of the new world organization.

Dave Breger, who claimed to have coined the term "GI Joe," was an Army artist who frequently satirized the bewildering bureaucracy of military life in his comic panel. Above, "Private Breger" is given a typical order of the day: "Arrange these documents alphabetically and then burn them."

The conferees also expanded their earlier decisions on postwar Germany. It had already been determined that an Inter-Allied Control Commission would supervise the occupation of the Reich by Allied troops and that Germany would be disarmed and compelled to pay reparations. The Soviet Union, ravaged by the German invasion, wanted to impose a harsh peace. While the British and the Americans would not agree to all the Soviet demands, they did go a long way toward making the Germans pay for the grief they had caused.

It was decided that East Prussia should be divided between Russia and Poland. No fixed sum was set for reparations, but Roosevelt and Churchill accepted as the basis for future discussion a Soviet proposal calling for a total of $20 billion, half to go to the U.S.S.R.

The Polish question, still bothersome, was the biggest single issue before the conference. Westerners had been disturbed when in August 1944 the Poles had risen against the Nazis in Warsaw, and the Soviet Army, only a few miles away, had permitted the rebels to be wiped out. The U.S.S.R. appeared bent on eliminating all political elements in Eastern Europe that were not subservient to Moscow. At Yalta neither Roosevelt nor Churchill would accede to Stalin's demand that their countries recognize the Soviet-fostered Lublin government. Instead, under Anglo-American pressure, Stalin agreed that the Lublin government should be reorganized to include democratic leaders and that free elections would be held at an early date. Democratic governments also were promised for the other countries liberated from the Nazis.

Most of Roosevelt's military advisers urged him to use the Yalta meeting to secure a firm pledge from the Soviet Union that it would enter the war against Japan. Some feared that Stalin would wait until the United States had bled itself in a costly invasion of Japan's home islands and then enter the war at the last moment to reap the benefits. To prevent this, Roosevelt negotiated a secret agreement with Stalin, approved by Churchill. In return for Russia's promise to enter the war against Japan within a few months of the German surrender, the President agreed that the Soviet Union should recover all it had lost in the Russo-Japanese War and approved the transfer of the Kurile Islands and the southern half of Sakhalin Island from Japan to Russia. The U.S.S.R. recognized Chinese suzerainty in Manchuria and agreed to conclude a treaty of amity and alliance with the Nationalist government of Chiang Kai-shek.

During the war Milton Caniff, already famous for "Terry and the Pirates," also drew the popular "Male Call." Miss Lace, the siren of his new series, appeared regularly in more than 3,000 service newspapers. Along with Rita Hayworth and Betty Grable, she became a favorite Army pin-up girl.

Fᴏʀ many years afterward the Yalta agreements would remain a subject of controversy in the West. Certainly some of the decisions made at the conference are open to criticism. Roosevelt seems to have had too much faith that his personal charm could beguile Stalin and too little insight into Soviet ruthlessness. It is questionable whether the United States should have underwritten Russia's demands in the Far East; Roosevelt should have demanded more specific understandings on Eastern Europe as well.

Nevertheless, the effect of the Yalta agreements was greatly exaggerated by postwar critics. Save for the Kuriles, the U.S.S.R. got nothing at Yalta that it did not already hold or could not easily acquire. It is true that the concessions in the Far East rested on a miscalculation of Japan's ability to carry on a prolonged war. However, this miscalculation was evidence not of subversion, as critics later said, but of an understandable concern about a foe that was offering bitter resistance in the Pacific. When the Polish story ended unhappily with a Communist regime imposed by Russia, it was not because of the Yalta agreements, but because these agreements were not carried out.

In addition to his desire to secure Russian participation in the war against Japan, Roosevelt at Yalta was determined to avoid disputes that might cause the Soviets to balk at the creation of a new world organization. If there were defects in the current settlements, the President counted on the new body to straighten them out after the war.

George Baker's dismal dogface, Sad Sack, was, according to Baker, the soldier "who works hard and then watches someone else get the promotion." Sad Sack's only lasting promotion was civilian: He was listed in several dictionaries and defined in one as "a hopelessly inept person; a ludicrous misfit."

Meanwhile events on the battlefield were still having their own effect on postwar diplomacy. As the Big Three headed home from Yalta, Anglo-American forces were advancing toward the Rhine. On March 7, 1945, by a great stroke of good fortune, American troops captured the Ludendorff Bridge at Remagen before it could be destroyed. Allies poured into the German heartland. German resistance crumpled as the British under Montgomery swept across the northern plain and, with Bradley's American forces, trapped more than 250,000 German soldiers in the Ruhr. In a matter of days American troops might be in Berlin. But instead of seizing the opportunity to take the German capital, Eisenhower, supported by the Joint Chiefs of Staff, sent his troops against the "National Redoubt" which Hitler was supposed to have readied for a last stand in the Bavarian and Austrian mountains.

Even after the "National Redoubt" proved to be a myth, the American forces were restrained. When American troops reached the Elbe, they halted there, only 53 miles from Berlin, and waited for the Russians to take the German capital. Churchill's plea "that we should shake hands with the Russians as far to the east as possible" was dismissed by American commanders, who spurned "political" decisions. Neither a seriously ill Roosevelt nor the poorly briefed Harry S. Truman, who succeeded to the presidency that April, saw fit to countermand the generals. "In this melancholy void," said Churchill, "one President could not act and the other could not know."

When at last Eisenhower decided to send Patton to capture Prague in Eastern Europe, a strong Soviet protest caused him to pull back. While the Americans waited, the Russians seized Prague and sealed the postwar fate of Czechoslovakia. In retrospect critics would argue that the United States should have captured both Berlin and Prague and then should have kept a large military force on an advanced eastern line until Russia honored its pledges. But at the time, there was little support for risking the lives of American soldiers to achieve political objectives.

O N April 25 American and Russian soldiers embraced near the town of Torgau on the western bank of the Elbe. In the next days events moved like a rushing torrent. Italian partisans killed Mussolini and strung him up by his heels alongside his mistress in a gasoline station in Milan. Adolf Hitler committed suicide in his bunker in Berlin. On May 4 at Brenner Pass, the United States Fifth Army, coming up through Italy, met the Seventh Army, coming down from Austria. At 2:41 a.m., May 7, at Eisenhower's headquarters in Rheims, Colonel General Alfred Jodl unconditionally surrendered the remnants of the German forces. The long-awaited day of victory in Europe —V-E Day—had come at last.

The triumph, as Churchill later wrote, was married to tragedy. As the fighting came to an end the Soviet Union, abruptly reversing its posture of co-operation, imposed a Communist government on Rumania and refused to honor its promises on Poland. As Churchill moved amid the cheering crowds on V-E Day, smiling and holding up two fingers in his famous "V for Victory" sign, it was "with an aching heart and a mind oppressed by forebodings."

Less than four weeks before, on April 12, 1945, in Warm Springs, Georgia, Franklin Roosevelt had died of a massive cerebral hemorrhage. Americans everywhere were stunned; it was hard to believe that the dynamic man who had been President for 12 years was suddenly gone. Women stood in the streets

Joe Rosenthal's photograph of the raising of the American flag atop Mount Suribachi on Iwo Jima is symbolic of the agony of triumph in that grinding battle and in the long Pacific war. Marines had to fight for five days to take the peak. Bringing fame to the photographer, and a Pulitzer Prize, the dramatic picture served as a model for a number of war memorials.

and wept; men who heard the news on their way home from work numbly shared the loss with strangers. Said the New York *Times,* "Men will thank God on their knees, a hundred years from now, that Franklin D. Roosevelt was in the White House."

Grief for the departed President mingled with anxiety over the war in the Pacific, where the Americans had begun the bloody campaign to close in on Japan's home islands. On February 19, 1945, Marine shock troops landed on Iwo Jima, a tiny island on the invasion route to Japan. In the first week the Marines captured the extinct volcano of Mount Suribachi and raised an American flag atop it, but the hardest fighting still lay ahead. The island was fortified with pillboxes, land mines, antitank barriers and sniper nests. The Japanese, in caves dug into the hard lava, sold their lives dearly in the fiercest kind of hand-to-hand combat.

On April 1, two weeks after Iwo fell, the largest invading force of the Pacific war landed on the island of Okinawa, only 350 miles southwest of Japan. The Japanese fought fanatically. Suicide airplane attacks sank many American ships and damaged others—but at a cost of 3,500 Japanese aircraft. American losses in land fighting were also high. On June 21, when Okinawa was secured, Americans counted nearly 50,000 casualties.

But by now the real threat to Japan—although neither the Japanese nor most Americans were aware of it—was scientific. The services of American scientists had been called upon to an extent never before known in the nation's history. Under Dr. Vannevar Bush, the Office of Scientific Research and Development had achieved remarkable results in many fields. Scientists had

THE ISLAND ROAD
TO JAPAN

To win advanced bases for an assault on Japan, the Allies began a two-pronged island-hopping campaign. In the Southwest Pacific the Marines invaded the Solomons (1). General MacArthur's forces fought up the New Guinea coast; their landing in the Philippines led to the naval battle of Leyte Gulf (2). In the Central Pacific Admiral Nimitz's command took Tarawa (3), the Marshalls and the Marianas; and after aiding the Philippine invasion, it seized Iwo Jima and Okinawa. A B-29 from Tinian (4) signaled the war's end with the Hiroshima atom bomb.

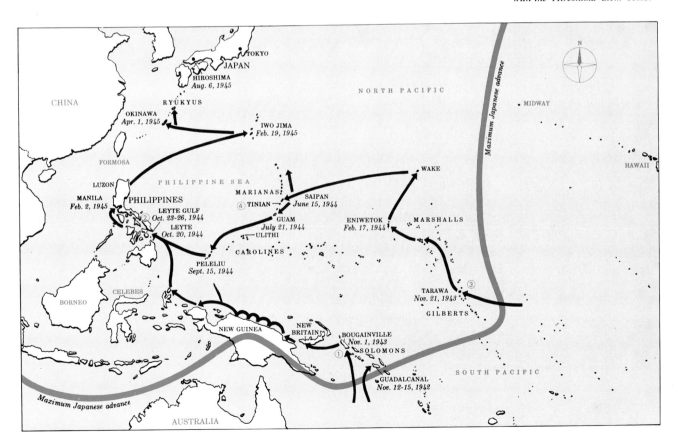

developed many new weapons, notably the rocket-launching "bazooka," with which two infantrymen could destroy a tank, and the proximity fuse, which used radio waves to detonate a shell as it neared its target.

By far the greatest of the new weapons grew from small beginnings abroad. On January 25, 1939, Niels Bohr, a Danish physicist, announced that two Germans at Berlin's Kaiser Wilhelm Institute had succeeded in achieving atomic fission in uranium. This development made feasible the construction of a bomb infinitely more deadly than any known to man. Albert Einstein was selected as spokesman by a group of American scientists to bring to President Roosevelt's attention the significance of this event and to urge that the United States initiate research into the implications of atomic fission.

Early in 1940 an American atomic program was started. At the University of California at Berkeley Dr. Ernest Lawrence, using a mighty cyclotron, or "atom smasher," found a way to produce fissionable material in substantial quantities. On December 2, 1942, the Italian-born physicist Enrico Fermi presided over the first controlled nuclear chain reaction in an improvised laboratory under the University of Chicago football stadium.

But enormous technical problems had yet to be solved. Control of production was turned over to the Manhattan District of the Corps of Engineers under General Leslie Groves. Groves selected two uninhabited sites for plants to make fissionable material. Overnight one of these spots, Hanford, Washington, became a tarpaper metropolis with 51,000 citizens. The other, Oak Ridge, with some 75,000, became the fifth largest city in Tennessee.

Yet so well was the secret of the project kept that hardly more than a dozen people in all the country knew the full details. Close-mouthed scientists would not even tell their families what they were doing. After working on the project for two years, Professor H. D. Smyth, chairman of Princeton's Department of Physics, was asked by his wife: "Why don't you get into some work which is really important, instead of traveling back and forth across the country on this vague business of yours?"

In the spring of 1943 at Los Alamos, New Mexico, American and European scientists began work on the bomb itself, under the direction of Dr. J. Robert Oppenheimer. On July 16, 1945, scientists and military men wearing dark glasses gathered before dawn on the New Mexico desert at Alamogordo. At the end of a countdown, the first atomic bomb was detonated. A blinding flash illuminated the desert, "a great green supersun," said newsman William L. Laurence, "climbing in a fraction of a second to a height of more than eight thousand feet, rising ever higher until it touched the clouds, lighting up earth and sky all around with a dazzling luminosity." A great column rose from the ground, eventually taking the mushroom shape that was to symbolize the new age. Then came a wave of intense heat, a thunderous roar and the trembling of the earth as though shaken by an earthquake. A scientist said: "I am sure that at the end of the world—in the last millisecond of the earth's existence—the last man will see something very similar to what we have seen."

PRESIDENT TRUMAN now faced a fateful decision. The bomb was such a horrendous weapon that some scientists urged that the United States conduct a public test demonstration as a warning before dropping it on a real target; perhaps it need not be used in the war. Some military men were sure that Japan was on the verge of surrender anyhow (a later survey by the U.S.

Dr. Vannevar Bush, head of the Office of Scientific Research and Development, is seen with a device symbolizing an OSRD development—radar-directed antiaircraft fire. The agency also developed new bombs and speeded penicillin production. Said Bush, "If we had been on our toes in war technology ten years ago, we would probably not have had this damn war."

Strategic Bombing Survey seemed to bear this out). But most of the President's advisers believed that Japan was still a formidable foe. The only alternative to dropping the A-bomb, they reasoned, was an invasion which might cost as many as a million casualties. A civilian committee recommended that the bomb be used as soon as possible on a joint military-civilian target, without prior warning.

Truman was determined to avoid an Okinawa from one end of Japan to the other. On July 26 he and Clement Attlee, who had just succeeded Churchill as Prime Minister of Britain, called upon Japan to surrender or face "the utter devastation of the Japanese homeland." The ultimatum was ignored.

On the morning of August 6, 1945, a single atomic bomb was dropped on the city of Hiroshima. Almost 68,000 were killed, with as many injured. That morning the dreadfully burned survivors moved through the flattened, eerily silent city, holding their arms out before them to prevent the seared surfaces from touching. That afternoon people who seemed to have escaped unharmed died, the first victims of radiation. Nevertheless, Japan did not sue for peace.

On August 9, a few hours after Russia had declared war on Japan, a second atomic bomb was exploded over Nagasaki; 38,000 were killed. Even then, Japanese leaders balked at surrender. The Emperor had to override his two chief military advisers in order to accept surrender terms.

A T last, almost four years after it began, the fighting in the Pacific had ended. World War II was over. On August 14, V-J Day, Americans celebrated the glad tidings. Across the country people poured into the streets, rang church bells, put on wild parades, loosed storms of confetti from office windows. In New York by 10 p.m. two million people had crowded into Times Square—a great sea of shouting, kissing, horn-blowing celebrants. In San Francisco sailors on shore leave staged a three-day riot; street cars were overturned, bond booths were ripped down and every window on lower Market Street was broken.

On September 2 an Allied armada sailed into Tokyo Bay. The tense Japanese representatives, maintaining their composure with difficulty, boarded the U.S.S. *Missouri*, the world's largest battleship, and walked the gantlet of stern-faced Allied officers. MacArthur signed the surrender document ceremoniously. The first two pens he handed to officers who had been rescued from Japanese prison camps only a few days before: Jonathan Wainwright, who had been forced to surrender Corregidor, and British Lieutenant General Arthur Ernest Percival, the ill-starred commander of Singapore. When the frosty ceremonies ended, the bosun's pipe marched the Japanese down over the side.

The war in the Pacific, a war fought with barbaric ferocity, was officially at an end, but only after years of horror climaxed by the revelation of what was called, with painful precision, "the ultimate weapon." From the *Missouri*, MacArthur, speaking by radio to the American people, underscored the inescapable moral: "A new era is upon us. . . . Men since the beginning of time have sought peace. . . . Military alliances, balances of power, leagues of nations, all in turn failed, leaving the only path to be by the way of the crucible of war. The utter destructiveness of war now blots out this alternative. We have had our last chance. If we do not devise some greater and more equitable system, Armageddon will be at our door."

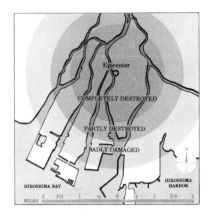

HIROSHIMA: A CITY DIES
GIVING BIRTH TO AN ERA

At exactly 8:15 a.m. on August 6, 81 per cent of the city of Hiroshima ceased to exist. One bomb, dubbed "Little Boy," exploded with the force of 20,000 tons of TNT. For an instant temperatures at the epicenter (above ground zero) were millions of degrees. Even a mile away many people suffered burns through their clothes. Factories, hospitals and homes disappeared. Buildings not in the area of total annihilation were damaged by the shock wave or destroyed by fire. Said one survivor: "Every living thing was blackened and dead—or waiting to die."

PRISONERS OF WAR, U.S. soldiers, hands bound behind them, rest on the 85-mile Bataan "death march." On the way, hundreds died of exhaustion and brutality. The Philippines fell in May 1942; it was months before the Allies could take the offensive.

A hundred beachheads to Tokyo

GEOGRAPHY shaped the war in the Pacific with an iron hand. Even before the fall of Bataan, it was clear that the only way to bring the fighting home to the enemy was by a slow, grinding advance from island to island until Japan itself was within striking distance. Those Pacific islands *(map, page 151)* were a horror. Marines and GIs who fought in New Guinea and the Solomons found the foul, murky rain forests *(opposite)* as implacable a foe as the Japanese soldier. Then, having learned—under fire—to survive in the jungle, they had to take new on-the-job training on the flat coral strands of Eniwetok and Kwajalein. And on the rugged honeycombed heights of Saipan and Iwo Jima, even the most knowledgeable veterans of jungle and atoll found they were novices all over again.

The Pacific war was powerfully influenced also by the tremendous distances between battlegrounds. In these sea wastes, fleets clashed in mighty contests that were largely dominated by aircraft carriers. The U.S. opened up more than 100 far-flung beachheads in the Pacific, 68 of them hotly contested. Each campaign required a bewildering variety of specialized arms, equipment and personnel. To help coordinate all of these elements for scores of D-days and H-hours, commands were streamlined, joint operations planned, complex new supply systems evolved. It was through these intricate channels, on a prodigious wave of matériel, that the men with rifles ultimately rode to victory.

PRISONERS OF GEOGRAPHY, U.S. troops stealthily advance on Guadalcanal; in such dense jungle, men knew "we would never get out unless we fought our way out.

The flattops: spearheads and targets of attack

B Y chance, U.S. aircraft carriers were absent from Pearl Harbor on December 7, 1941, when their full value was proved by the carrier-based Japanese attack that knocked out much of the U.S. Pacific Fleet. At first outnumbered 10 to 3, American flattops struck back boldly. Their planes softened up islands to be invaded, supported assault troops and later bombed Japan itself.

The U.S.S. *Hornet*, which launched the famous first raid on Tokyo *(below)*, went on to fight in the tide-turning battle of Midway. It made its last attack off the Santa Cruz Islands *(top, right)* in October 1942, when, after absorbing tremendous punishment, it went to the bottom. But a new carrier bearing its proud name came out to meet the mounting threat of Nippon's kamikaze corps. Japanese pilots by the hundreds, seeking a death "as sudden and clean as the shattering of crystal," aimed their planes at U.S. warships. As many as one in four hit home, but the new *Hornet* managed to stay intact. Soon it helped to carry the war to Japan's very doorstep.

The carrier "Hornet," shown burning at center, is attacked by an

The new "Hornet," commissioned 13 months after its namesake

TAKING OFF from the *Hornet*, one of Lieutenant Colonel James Doolittle's 16 B-25s wings toward Tokyo 668 miles away. The 1942 raid caused little damage but boosted U.S. morale.

156

enemy plane in the battle of Santa Cruz. Japan's losses—100 planes plus the use of two carriers—shattered plans to retake Guadalcanal.

was sunk (above), narrowly escapes a kamikaze in 1945. At Okinawa alone, suicide planes hit over 300 U.S. ships, killing thousands.

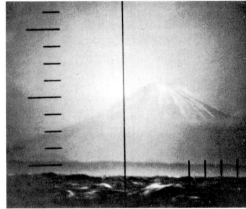

SACRED MOUNT FUJI looms up in a periscope view of the Japanese coast taken by a U.S. sub in 1943.

Rapier thrusts of the Navy's "silent service"

For those 16,000 Americans who saw Pacific service on some 200 submarines, the war was a round of terrible tensions. There was the loneliness of long night watches *(left);* the peril of reconnoitering enemy shores *(above);* the stress of patrols that kept 80-man crews confined in tiny quarters for weeks (the average was 47 days); and, late in the war, there was the unnerving wait to rescue those airmen forced down on bombing missions. But the chief work of the "silent service" was destruction. Of eight million tons of Japanese shipping sunk in the war, U.S. underseas craft accounted for fully 58 per cent—more than 1,200 ships. And they were responsible for nearly one third of the Imperial Navy's losses as well.

GIs hit the beach at Rendova in the Solomons, June 1943. Army units were generally employed to exploit the gains of Marine assault troops.

In the jungle, "fury by day and terror by night"

THE rain forests of the Southwest Pacific spawned a brand of warfare new to Americans. "It was a sly and sneaky kind of combat," said Lieutenant General Robert Eichelberger, whose victory at Buna Mission in New Guinea produced the grim scenes at left and opposite. "When the rains came, wounded men might drown before the litter bearers found them. Many did." The Japanese sniped from treetops, infiltrated by dark and blew themselves up rather than surrender. And, as Major Frank Hough wrote of the fighting in New Britain, there was "always the rain and the mud, torrid heat and teeming insect life, the stink of rotten jungle and rotting dead; malaria burning the body and fungus infection eating away the feet.... And fury by day and terror by night and utter weariness all the time. And death."

KILLED IN ACTION, American soldiers lie where they fell on Buna beach. This picture, released after the six-month campaign ended on January 2, 1943, shocked the nation.

DYING IN DEFIANCE, a Japanese who refused to surrender sprawls before the GI who had to shoot him. His death at Buna Mission came the day after fighting ended.

Swarms of ships ride at anchor in Ulithi atoll, a major hub of Pacific naval operations by October 1944. On islands around the lagoon

Hard-won island bases for a mounting U.S. assault

IN 1944 the U.S. island-hopping campaign shifted into high gear and closed in on Japan from the south and the east. As island groups fell, the Navy's Seabees and the Army's Corps of Engineers swiftly built vast bases for the operations to follow. Ulithi atoll in the Carolines, destined to be the main feeder base for the reconquest of the Philippines, was seized on September 23. Soon its sprawling oval lagoon *(above)* sheltered hundreds of ships at a time. Eventually the Navy developed tender-

were an airstrip, a hospital and a rest area for war-weary seamen.

A HUSKY SEABEE hammers coral into sand to enlarge a B-24 airstrip on Eniwetok. These tough builders began work so soon after invasion that they often had to fight off attacks.

A GIANT SUPERFORT, the war's biggest bomber, stands poised on its Guam runway in the Marianas. The B-29s arrived in a mass migration from California via Hawaii and Kwajalein.

and-tanker fleets as huge "floating bases" that enabled the warships to stay at sea almost indefinitely.

By December, four months after the Marianas were secured, runways had been built on Saipan for 180 B-29s. By the end of the year these huge bombers were flying missions over Japan. To gain an emergency landing field for them, and also a base for fighter escorts, a great armada assembled in the Marianas to invade an ugly little island halfway to Japan: Iwo Jima *(next page)*.

Priceless isles of rubble

To a Japanese defender, Iwo Jima was "an island of sulphur, no water, no sparrow, and no swallow." To the U.S. Marines, it was one solid fort of eight square miles covered with black sand and volcanic rubble. When Iwo lay strewn with mangled bodies and smashed matériel, as pictured below, a wounded

Marine said fervently, "I hope to God that we don't have to go on any more of those screwy islands!"

Iwo's network of concrete pillboxes and honeycombed hills was barely dented by 73 days of bombardment. After the Marines poured ashore on February 19, 1945, they bogged down in innumerable small, vicious battles. Agonizingly, they knocked out Japanese strong points one by one, using flame throwers and dynamite. Finally, on March 16, Iwo was secured; the Marines counted 6,000 dead, 17,000 wounded. Ahead lay Okinawa, the last of "those screwy islands" on the road to Japan.

Mushroom clouds and the blessed "hush of history"

Last-ditch enemy resistance on Iwo Jima and Okinawa convinced U.S. officials that a half-million Americans might die in an invasion of Japan. Hoping to preclude such losses, President Harry S. Truman sent a fateful order to a special bomber group in the Marianas. On August 6, 1945, a B-29 dropped an atomic bomb that all but obliterated Hiroshima. Three days later, a second awesome cloud rose over Nagasaki (below). On August 14 hostilities ended.

On September 2 victors and vanquished gathered on the U.S. battleship *Missouri* in Tokyo Bay. Amidst what one observer called "the hush of history," General Umezu signed (right) to complete Japan's surrender. Three years eight months and 26 days after Pearl Harbor, the war was over.

"THE ULTIMATE WEAPON," an atomic bomb, raises a great mushroom cloud above Nagasaki on August 9. In 24 days, peace dawned on a new, more dangerous world.

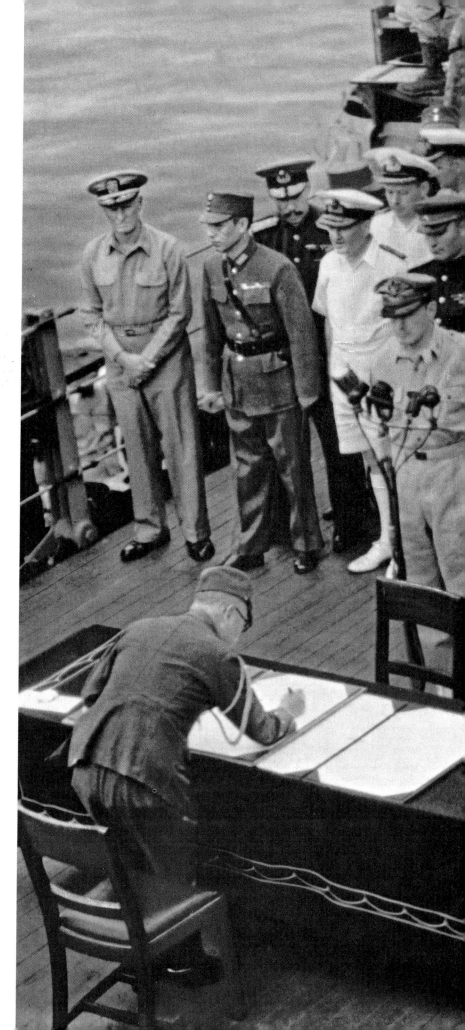

CHRONOLOGY *A timetable of American and world events: 1933-1945*

WORLD EVENTS	FOREIGN AFFAIRS	POLITICS	ECONOMICS and SCIENCE	THOUGHT and CULTURE	WORLD WAR II
1933 Hitler comes to power in Germany	1933 Roosevelt announces a "Good Neighbor" policy toward Latin America	1933-45 Franklin D. Roosevelt President	1933 Banking panic precedes Roosevelt inauguration	1933 First All-Star Baseball Game played	Sept. 1939 German invasion of Poland leads to Franco-British declaration of war
1933 Germany leaves League of Nations	1933 London Economic Conference fails to promote international co-operation	1933-46 Democrats control both houses of Congress	1933 Unemployment reaches an estimated 13 million	1933 Caldwell's *God's Little Acre* and Joyce's *Ulysses* freed from obscenity charges	April-May 1940 Hitler overruns Norway, Denmark, the Low Countries and France
1934 U.S.S.R. admitted to League of Nations	1933 United States recognizes the U.S.S.R.	1933 20th (Lame Duck) Amendment ratified; 21st Amendment ends prohibition	1933 U.S. abandons gold standard and devaluates currency	1934 Catholic Legion of Decency begins rating moral quality of motion pictures	May-June 1940 British troops evacuate Dunkirk
1934 Alexander I of Yugoslavia assassinated on state visit to France	1934 Vinson-Trammel Act permits building of full treaty quota of capital ships	1933 First Hundred Days: establishment of numerous New Deal agencies including CCC, FERA, AAA, TVA, HOLC, FDIC, NRA, CWA	1933-36 Severe droughts turn Great Plains into "Dust Bowl"	1934 onward Odets, Hellman, Sherwood and others write popular plays of social criticism	June 1940 French sign armistice with Germany
1934 Luigi Pirandello of Italy wins Nobel Prize in Literature	1934 Tydings-McDuffie Act pledges Philippine independence by 1945	1934 Anti-New Deal, ultraconservative American Liberty League formed	1934 Gold Reserve Act stabilizes the dollar	1935 Premiere of George Gershwin's *Porgy and Bess*	Aug. 1940-June 1941 Britain withstands Germany's bombing attacks
1934 First meeting of Hitler and Mussolini, in Venice	1934 Johnson Act prohibits loans to nations defaulting on debts to U.S.	1934 New Deal legislation: Export-Import Bank, Cotton Control Act, SEC, FHA, Corporate Bankruptcy Act, FCC, Silver Purchase Act	1934 Harold C. Urey wins Nobel Prize in Chemistry	1935 Sinclair Lewis' *It Can't Happen Here* published	Sept. 1940 Japan occupies Indochina, joins Axis
1934 Premiere of Shostakovich opera *Lady Macbeth of Minsk*, later denounced by Stalin	1934-36 Revelations of Nye Munitions Investigation help promote isolationism	1935 Supreme Court upholds 1933 gold legislation, invalidates National Industrial Recovery Act	1934 Trade Agreements Act permits tariff cuts	1935 James T. Farrell completes *Studs Lonigan* trilogy	Oct.-Dec. 1940 Italians repulsed in attempted invasion of Greece
1934 Hitler purges Nazi leadership	1935 Neutrality Act embargoes sale of arms and other materials to belligerents, forbids U.S. travel on belligerent vessels	1935 Assassination of Huey Long	1934 Violent strikes and labor agitation	1935-39 "Popular Front" era of American Communist party	Dec. 1940-April 1941 British offensive in North Africa
1934-38 Purges within the Russian Communist party	1935 Congress defeats proposal that U.S. join the World Court	1935 Second Hundred Days: NLRA, Social Security Act, Wealth Tax Act, Banking Act, Public Utility Holding Company Act, Guffey-Snyder Coal Act passed; other New Deal agencies created	1934-40 Development of military radar systems	1935-39 WPA Federal Theater Project	April-May 1941 Germans defeat British in North Africa
1935 Hitler prisoner, Carl von Ossietzky, wins Nobel Peace Prize			1935 Industrial unionists within AFL form Committee for Industrial Organization		June 1941 Germany invades the Soviet Union
1935 Saar returned to Germany after plebiscite			1935 Edwin Armstrong demonstrates FM radio		1941-Jan. 1943 Siege of Leningrad
1935 Hitler proclaims anti-Semitic laws					Sept. 1941 U.S. supplies naval cover for convoys, arms merchant ships; after sinkings by German U-boats, declares that it will "shoot at sight" in the North Atlantic
1935-36 Italy invades and occupies Ethiopia, ignoring League of Nations sanctions					Dec. 7, 1941 Japanese attack on Pearl Harbor

1936 A Roosevelt Landslide

WORLD EVENTS	FOREIGN AFFAIRS	POLITICS	ECONOMICS and SCIENCE	THOUGHT and CULTURE	WORLD WAR II
1936 Germany remilitarizes the Rhineland	1937 Neutrality Act adds cash-and-carry provision	1936 Anti-New Deal coalition of extremists Townsend, Coughlin, Smith	1936 Merchant Marine Act provides government aid to shipping	1936 Eugene O'Neill wins Nobel Prize in Literature	Dec. 1941 U.S. declares war on Japan, Germany and Italy
1936 Edward VIII of England abdicates	1937 Roosevelt quarantine-of-aggressors speech	1936 Supreme Court invalidates Agricultural Adjustment Act	1936-39 Major testing of sulfa drugs	1936 Margaret Mitchell's *Gone With the Wind* published	Dec. 1941 Japanese capture Guam, Wake, Hong Kong, invade Malaya
1936-39 Spanish Civil War	1937 Japanese bomb U.S. gunboat *Panay* in Chinese waters	1936 Soil Conservation and Domestic Allotment Act	1937 Auto industry largely unionized by sit-down strikes	1936 John Dos Passos completes *U.S.A.* trilogy	Jan.-March 1942 Japanese capture Manila, Singapore, occupy Netherlands East Indies
1936-52 George VI king of England	1938 Declaration of Lima pledges resistance of 21 Hemisphere nations to Fascism and foreign intervention	1936 Roosevelt re-elected President by landslide	1937 La Follette report on antilabor techniques	1937 First Disney full-length cartoon, *Snow White*	Feb.-March 1942 Heavy American losses in battle of Java Sea
1937 Japanese begin undeclared war in China	1938 Defeat of Ludlow resolution for national referendum in case of war	1937 Congress defeats Roosevelt's Supreme Court reorganization plan	1937-38 Sharp recession interrupts gradual business recovery	1937 N.B.C. Symphony Orchestra created for Toscanini	April-May 1942 Bataan and Corregidor fall
1938 Hitler takes Austria	1938-47 Controversy over expropriation of U.S. property by Mexico	1937 Supreme Court upholds a variety of New Deal measures, including the NLRA and Social Security Act	1938 Commercial production of nylon begun	1937-49 Joe Louis heavyweight champion of the world	May 1942 Japanese fleet withdraws after battle of Coral Sea
1938 Nazis take violent anti-Jewish measures in Germany	1939 Arms embargo to belligerents repealed; cash-and-carry provisions extended to arms	1937 Guffey-Vinson Coal Act, Farm Tenancy Act, Wagner-Steagall National Housing Act passed	1938 Industrial unionists formally organize Congress of Industrial Organizations (CIO)	1938 Aaron Copland's ballet *Billy the Kid* performed	June 1942 Japanese suffer first major defeat at Midway
1938 Enrico Fermi of Italy wins Nobel Prize in Physics	1939 Panama Congress establishes wide security zone around the Americas	1938 House Committee on Un-American Activities established	1938 Civil Aeronautics Administration established	1938 Pearl S. Buck wins Nobel Prize in Literature	Aug. 1942 U.S. takes offensive in Solomon Islands
1938-39 Germany presides over dismemberment of Czechoslovakia	1939 Scientists inform Roosevelt of possibility of making an atomic bomb and of very real danger that Germany might be	1938 Second AAA, Fair Labor Standards Act mark the end of New Deal reform legislation	1938-40 Strong antitrust campaign	1938 "Invasion from Mars" broadcast by Orson Welles, creates near-panic	Aug. 1942-Feb. 1943 Battle of Stalingrad
April 1939 Italian invasion of Albania		1938 Roosevelt suffers humiliating defeat in his attempt at purging conservative Democrats	1938-41 Temporary National Economic Committee investigates trends of the economy	1939 Golden Gate International Exposition at San Francisco	Oct.-Nov. 1942 British clear Egypt of Axis troops
Aug. 1939 Hitler and Stalin conclude Russo-German Nonaggression Pact		1939 Hatch Act prohibits federal employees from participation in	1939-45 World War II brings economic boom, ends unemployment	1939 Baseball Hall of Fame dedicated at Cooperstown	Nov. 1942 Operation TORCH: Allied invasion of North Africa
Nov. 1939 Russia invades Finland				1939 John Steinbeck's *Grapes of Wrath* published	Nov. 1942 Germans occupy Vichy France; French fleet scuttled
1939-58 Pius XII serves as Pope					

1940 Destroyers for Bases

1940 Leon Trotsky, exiled Russian leader, assassinated in Mexico
1940 Russia annexes the Baltic republics of Estonia, Latvia and Lithuania
May 1940-July 1945 Winston Churchill British prime minister
June 1940 Italy enters war as German ally
June 1940 Russia invades the Baltic republics
1940-44 Pétain dictatorship in Vichy France
1941 Penicillin's use on human beings first reported
April 1941 Russo-Japanese Neutrality Pact
1941-44 Tojo government in Japan

1940 Pittman Resolution authorizes sale of arms to the nations of the Western Hemisphere
1940 Destroyers-for-bases deal with Britain
1940 Hull warns Japan against invasion of East Indies and Indochina
1940 U.S. declares embargo on iron and steel scrap
1940 Burke-Wadsworth Act creates selective service
1940 President asks for bipartisan foreign policy, names Republican Secretaries of Navy and War
1940 National Defense Research Committee, Office of Production Management created
Jan. 1941 Roosevelt "Four Freedoms" speech defines anti-Fascist impulse
March 1941 Lend-lease agreement approved
April-July 1941 U.S. occupation of Greenland and Iceland
July 1941 Japanese credits in U.S. frozen
Aug. 1941 Atlantic Charter proclaimed
Nov. 1941 U.S. extends a $1 billion lend-lease credit to Russia
Nov. 1941 U.S. ambassador to Japan warns of possible surprise attack in the Pacific
Nov. 1941 Secretary of State Hull offers Japan a 10-point program to settle differences in the Far East
Jan. 1942 United Nations Pact signed by 26 nations at Washington
Jan. 1942 Rio de Janeiro Pact pledges Latin-American opposition to Fascism

1940 Concern with foreign policy spawns rival aid-the-Allies and America-first pressure groups
1940 Alien Registration Act passed to counter subversive threat
1940 Roosevelt defeats Willkie for unprecedented third term
1940-45 Defense spending rises from annual $1.5 billion to $81.3 billion
1941 Supreme Court upholds Fair Labor Standards Act of 1938
1942-45 Pacific Coast Japanese relocated in Western concentration camps

1940 First demonstration of color television
1940 Census shows 131,669,275 inhabitants
1940-45 Gross farm income rises from annual $11 billion to $25.4 billion
1941 Fair Employment Practices Committee appointed
1941 Office of Scientific Research and Development established
1941 Office of Production Management, National Defense Mediation Board, Office of Price Administration formed to stabilize production, wages, salaries and prices
1942 First jet plane tests in U.S.
1942 Grand Coulee Dam completed
1942 First self-sustaining nuclear chain reaction achieved
1942 Alaska Highway constructed
1942-47 Rationing of various goods in short supply

1940 Thomas Wolfe's You Can't Go Home Again published posthumously
1940 Richard Wright's Native Son published
1942 Irving Berlin's "White Christmas" published
1942 L. C. Douglas' The Robe published

Solomons, offensives in southern and central Pacific
Feb.-May 1943 Defeat of Axis forces in North Africa
March 1943 Battle of Bismarck Sea
May-Aug. 1943 Japanese expelled from Aleutian Islands
July 1943 Allied landing in Sicily
July-Dec. 1943 Russians throw Germans back to Dnieper River
Sept. 1943 Allied landing at Salerno; Italy surrenders; Germans occupy Italy, rescue Mussolini
1943-45 American air power smashes at European targets

Feb. 1944 Invasion of the Marshalls: Eniwetok, Kwajalein
March-Aug. 1944 Allies advance to Florence, then stalled
May-Aug. 1944 Capture of Bougainville and Gilbert Islands
June 1944 Invasion of the Marianas: Saipan
June 1944 Operation OVERLORD: Allied landings at Normandy
Aug. 1944 Landings in southern France; liberation of Paris
Aug. 1944 U.S. recaptures Guam
Sept. 1944 V-2 bombings of London
Oct. 1944 Battle of Leyte Gulf; start of reconquest of Philippines
Nov. 1944 B-29s begin raids on Japan from Saipan
Dec. 1944 Battle of the Bulge

Jan.-Feb. 1945 Russians sweep through Poland
Feb. 1945 Ledo road from Burma to China opened
Feb. 1945 Americans enter Manila
Feb.-March 1945 Battle for Iwo Jima
March 1945 U.S. aircraft carriers penetrate Japanese home waters
March 1945 Rhine crossed at Remagen, U.S. troops take Cologne
April 1945 U.S. and Russian forces meet at Elbe
April 1945 German resistance in north Italy falters; Mussolini executed; Hitler a suicide
April-June 1945 Height of Japanese suicide attacks on U.S. ships

1943 "Unconditional Surrender"

May 1943 Stalin dissolves the Third Communist International
1944 Otto Hahn of Germany wins Nobel Prize in Chemistry
1944 International Red Cross wins Nobel Peace Prize for wartime work
Oct. 1944 De Gaulle's provisional government of France widely recognized
1945-51 Attlee Labour government in Britain

Aug. 1943 Quebec Conference recognizes French Committee of National Liberation
Jan. 1943 Casablanca Conference demands Axis "unconditional surrender"
Nov. 1943 Cairo Conference on Far East
Nov.-Dec. 1943 Teheran Conference on international organization
Feb. 1945 Yalta Conference
April-June 1945 San Francisco Conference creates U.N. Charter
1945 Potsdam Conference on Germany

1943 Congress passes Connally-Fulbright resolutions calling for bipartisan effort toward an international organization
1943-44 Army takes temporary possession of railroads to prevent strike
1944 Roosevelt defeats Dewey to win fourth term
1944 Supreme Court upholds exclusion of Japanese from Pacific Coast
1945 Roosevelt dies; succeeded by Vice President Harry S. Truman

1943 Office of War Mobilization established
1943 Discovery of streptomycin
1944 Total union membership of 14,146,000 is more than one third of nonagricultural labor force
1945 Testing and use of the atomic bomb

1943 Ernie Pyle's Here Is Your War published
1943 Betty Smith's A Tree Grows in Brooklyn published
1943 Wendell Willkie's One World published
1943 Rodgers and Hammerstein's Oklahoma! opens
1944 GI Bill of Rights enacted by Congress
1945 Tennessee Williams play The Glass Menagerie performed

April-June 1945 Battle for Okinawa
May 1945 Berlin falls
May 8, 1945 V-E day: Germany surrenders, is occupied by Four Powers
May-Aug. 1945 Systematic bombing of Japan
Aug. 1945 Russians declare war on Japan, invade Manchuria
Aug. 1945 Atomic bombs dropped on Hiroshima, Nagasaki
Aug. 14, 1945 V-J Day: Japan surrenders
Sept. 1945 Formal surrender signed on U.S.S. Missouri in Tokyo harbor; occupation of Japan

FOR FURTHER READING

These books were selected for their interest and authority in preparation of this volume and for their usefulness to readers seeking additional information on specific points. An asterisk (*) marks works available in both hard-cover and paperback editions; a dagger (†) indicates availability only in paperback.

GENERAL READING

*Burns, James MacGregor, *Roosevelt: The Lion and the Fox.* Harcourt, Brace & World, 1957.
Freidel, Frank, *America in the Twentieth Century.* Knopf, 1960.
*Leuchtenburg, William E., *Franklin D. Roosevelt and the New Deal, 1932-1940.* Harper & Row, 1963.
Moley, Raymond, *After Seven Years.* Harper & Row, 1939.
*Rauch, Basil, *The History of the New Deal, 1933-1938.* Creative Age Press, 1944.
Roosevelt, F. D., *The Public Papers and Addresses of F.D.R.* Vols. I-V, Random House, 1938; Vols. VI-IX, Macmillan, 1941; Vols. X-XIII, compiled by Samuel I. Rosenman. Harper & Row, 1950.
Schlesinger, Arthur M. Jr., *The Age of Roosevelt* (3 vols.). Houghton Mifflin, 1957-1960.
†Shannon, David (ed.), *The Great Depression.* Prentice-Hall, 1960.
Snyder, Louis L., *The War: A Concise History, 1939-1945.* Julian Messner, 1960.

THE FIRST HUNDRED DAYS (CHAPTER 1)

Bernstein, Irving, *The Lean Years.* Houghton Mifflin, 1960.
Blum, John M., *From the Morgenthau Diaries* (Vol. 1). Houghton Mifflin, 1959.
Johnson, Hugh, *The Blue Eagle from Egg to Earth.* Doubleday, 1935.
Lindley, Ernest, *The Roosevelt Revolution: First Phase.* Viking Press, 1933.
Mitchell, Broadus, *Depression Decade.* Rinehart, 1947.
Pagano, Grace, *Collection of Contemporary American Painting.* Encyclopaedia Britannica, 1946.
Rollins, A. B., *Roosevelt and Howe.* Knopf, 1962.
Wecter, Dixon, *The Age of the Great Depression.* Macmillan, 1948.

WELFARE STATE, ROOSEVELT MAGIC (CHAPTERS 2, 3)

*Allen, Frederick Lewis, *Since Yesterday.* Harper & Row, 1940.
*Bernstein, Irving, *New Deal Collective Bargaining Policy.* University of California, 1950.
Congdon, Don, *The Thirties, a Time to Remember.* Simon and Schuster, 1962.
Flanagan, Hallie, *Arena.* Duell, Sloan & Pearce, 1940.
Greer, Thomas, *What Roosevelt Thought.* Michigan State University Press, 1958.
Levinson, Edward, *Labor on the March.* Harper & Row, 1938.
McWilliams, Carey, *Ill Fares the Land.* Little, Brown, 1942.
Perkins, Frances, *The Roosevelt I Knew.* Viking Press, 1946.
*Sherwood, Robert E., *Roosevelt and Hopkins.* Harper & Row, 1948.
Stokes, Thomas L., *Chip off My Shoulder.* Princeton University Press, 1940.
Tugwell, Rexford Guy, *The Democratic Roosevelt.* Doubleday, 1957.

THE END OF THE NEW DEAL (CHAPTER 4)

Arnold, Thurman W., *The Bottlenecks of Business.* Reynal and Hitchcock, 1940.
*Arnold, Thurman W., *The Folklore of Capitalism.* Oxford University Press, 1937.
Brogan, D. W., *Era of Franklin D. Roosevelt.* Yale University Press, 1951.
Cox, James M., *Journey Through My Years.* Simon and Schuster, 1946.
Dies, Martin, *The Trojan Horse in America.* Dodd, Mead, 1940.
Eccles, Marriner, *Beckoning Frontiers.* Knopf, 1951.
Farley, James A., *Jim Farley's Story, Roosevelt Years.* McGraw-Hill, 1948.
Galenson, Walter, *The CIO Challenge to the AFL.* Harvard University Press, 1960.
Gosnell, Harold, *Champion Campaigner, Franklin D. Roosevelt.* Macmillan, 1952.
*Gunther, John, *Roosevelt in Retrospect.* Harper & Row, 1950.
Hacker, Louis, *A Short History of the New Deal.* F. S. Crofts, 1934.
Howe, Irving, and B. J. Widick, *The UAW and Walter Reuther.* Random House, 1949.
Ickes, Harold, *The Secret Diary of Harold Ickes* (3 vols.). Simon and Schuster, 1953-1954.

*Jackson, Robert H., *The Struggle for Judicial Supremacy.* Knopf, 1941.
Lubell, Samuel, *The Revolt of the Moderates.* Harper & Row, 1956.
Nevins, Allan, *The New Deal and World Affairs.* Yale University Press, 1950.
Ogden, August, *The Dies Committee.* The Catholic University of America Press, 1943.
*Perkins, Dexter, *The New Age of Franklin D. Roosevelt, 1932-45.* Chicago University Press, 1957.
Pritchett, Charles H., *The Roosevelt Court.* Macmillan, 1948.
Roose, Kenneth, *The Economics of Recession and Revival.* Yale University Press, 1954.
Roosevelt, Eleanor, *Autobiography.* Harper & Row, 1961.
Swisher, Carl, *American Constitutional Development.* Houghton Mifflin, 1954.

ON THE WORLD STAGE (CHAPTER 5)

Bailey, Thomas A., *Diplomatic History of the American People.* Appleton-Century-Crofts, 1958.
Browder, Robert Paul, *Origins of Soviet-American Diplomacy.* Princeton University Press, 1953.
Divine, Robert A., *The Illusion of Neutrality.* Chicago University Press, 1962.
Ferrell, Robert H., *American Diplomacy; a History.* Norton, 1959.
Goodman, Jack (ed.), *While You Were Gone.* Simon and Schuster, 1946.
Grew, Joseph C., *Turbulent Era.* Houghton Mifflin, 1952.
Hull, Cordell, *Memoirs* (Vols. 1 and 2). Macmillan, 1948.
Langer, William, and S. E. Gleason, *Challenge to Isolation.* Harper & Row, 1952.
McWilliams, Carey, *Prejudice. Japanese-Americans: symbol of racial intolerance.* Little, Brown, 1944.
Taylor, F. Jay, *The United States and the Spanish Civil War.* Bookman Associates, 1956.

THE WAR FOR SURVIVAL (CHAPTER 6)

Bradley, Omar Nelson, *A Soldier's Story.* Holt, Rinehart & Winston, 1951.
Craven, Wesley F., and James L. Cate (eds.), *The Army Air Forces in World War II* (7 vols.). University of Chicago Press, 1948-1958.
*Eisenhower, Dwight D., *Crusade in Europe.* Doubleday, 1948.
*Hersey, John, *Into the Valley.* Knopf, 1943.
Kenney, William, *The Crucial Years, 1940-1945.* MacFadden, 1963.
Link, Arthur S., and William B. Catton, *The American Epoch.* Knopf, 1963.
Menefee, Selden C., *Assignment: U.S.A.* Reynal & Hitchcock, 1943.
Merriam, Robert E., *Dark December.* Ziff-Davis Publishing Company, 1947.
Morison, Samuel Eliot, *History of the U.S. Naval Operations in World War II* (14 vols.). Little, Brown, 1947-1963.
*Toland, John, *But Not in Shame.* Random House, 1961.

THE GRAND ALLIANCE (CHAPTER 7)

*Brookhouser, Frank, *This Was Your War.* Doubleday, 1960.
Brown, John Mason, *To All Hands.* McGraw-Hill, 1943.
†Clagett, John, *The U.S. Navy in Action.* Monarch Books, 1963.
Commager, Henry S. (ed.), *The Story of the Second World War.* Little, Brown, 1945.
Feis, Herbert, *Between War and Peace: The Potsdam Conference.* Princeton University Press, 1960.
Feis, Herbert, *Churchill, Roosevelt, Stalin.* Princeton University Press, 1957.
Loomis, Robert D., *The Story of the U.S. Air Force.* Random House, 1959.
Miller, Francis Trevelyan, *History of World War II.* John C. Winston Co., 1945.
Monks, John Jr., *A Ribbon and a Star.* Holt, Rinehart & Winston, 1945.
*Pyle, Ernie, *Here Is Your War.* Holt, Rinehart & Winston, 1943.
Sherrod, Robert, *Tarawa.* Duell, Sloan & Pearce, 1944.
*Tregaskis, Richard, *Guadalcanal Diary.* Random House, 1943.
*Wilmot, Chester, *The Struggle for Europe.* Harper & Row, 1963.
Wolfert, Ira, *Battle for the Solomons.* Houghton Mifflin, 1943.

ACKNOWLEDGMENTS

The author wishes to acknowledge his deep indebtedness to Carol Moodie for research assistance and to Jean McIntire Leuchtenburg for editorial suggestions. The editors of this book are indebted to the following: James P. Shenton, Associate Professor of History, Columbia University; Thurman Arnold, Arnold, Fortas & Porter, Washington, D.C.; Edward Bryant, Assistant Curator, Whitney Museum of American Art, New York City; Dr. Elizabeth B. Drewry, Director, Franklin Delano Roosevelt Library, Hyde Park, New York; Mrs. Virginia G. Fincik and Mrs. Frances M. Lewis, pictorial researchers, Photographic Services, Department of the Air Force, Washington, D.C.; Robert A. Lovett, Brown Brothers, Harriman & Co., New York City; Mrs. Marian R. McNaughton, Museum Curator, DCSOPS Office Chief of Staff OCMH, Historical Service Division, Historical Properties Branch, Washington, D.C.; Miss Edith Midgette, Chief of the Magazine and Book Branch, Office of the Assistant Secretary of Defense (Public Affairs); Miss Josephine Motylewski, Archivist, Audio-Visual Branch, Office of Civil Archives, National Archives and Records Service, Washington, D.C.; Robert Sherrod, Editor-at-Large, Saturday Evening Post, New York City; Milton Kaplan and Carl Stange, Library of Congress, Washington, D.C.; and Judy Higgins.

PICTURE CREDITS

The sources for the illustrations in this book are shown below. Credits for pictures from left to right are separated by semicolons, top to bottom by dashes. Sources have been abbreviated as follows: Bettmann—The Bettmann Archive; Brown—Brown Brothers; Culver—Culver Pictures; LC—Library of Congress; NYPL—The New York Public Library; UPI—United Press International.

Cover—U.S. Army from Wide World Photos

End papers drawn by Thomas Vroman

CHAPTER 1: 6—Courtesy of Franklin D. Roosevelt Warm Springs Memorial Commission, Madame Elizabeth Shoumatoff, Artist. 8, 9—UPI; Brown. 10, 11—Culver; Gimbels Stamp Collection. 12, 13—Reprinted from *Vanity Fair*; copyright © 1933 by The Condé Nast Publications Inc. 14—Bottom: Culver. 16, 17—The Metropolitan Museum of Art, Gift of Mrs. Priscilla A. B. Henderson, 1950; collection of the Nebraska Art Association, Lincoln. 18, 19—Collection of Charles J. Rosenbloom; Eric Schaal, collection of Mrs. Max Weber, courtesy of The Downtown Gallery, New York—Isaac Soyer: *Employment Agency*. 1937. Collection of the Whitney Museum of American Art, New York. 20, 21—Collection of Earle Ludgin, acquired from The Downtown Gallery, New York, copied by Richard Brittain for FORTUNE—Robert Crandall, courtesy Armand G. Erpf; *Trouble in Frisco, 1938*. Detail from painting by Fletcher Martin. Collection, The Museum of Modern Art, New York, Mrs. John D. Rockefeller, Jr. Fund. 22, 23—Stewart Love, Museum of Art, Carnegie Institute, Pittsburgh, Pennsylvania; NYPL—Picture Collection. 24, 25—Top left: Collection of the Cincinnati Art Museum—collection Mr. and Mrs. Edward Marcus, acquired from The Downtown Gallery, copied by John Rogers; right: courtesy permanent collection, University of Arizona, copied by Ray Manley. 26, 27—*Feast of Pure Reason*. 1937. Detail from painting by Jack Levine. Collection, The Museum of Modern Art, New York, copied by Henry B. Beville; University of Rochester Memorial Art Gallery.

CHAPTER 2: 28—Courtesy LC. 30, 31—Wide World Photos except left R. A. Lewis in the Milwaukee *Journal*. 32—Culver—Brown. 33—Wide World Photos. 36, 37—Courtesy LC; Culver. 38, 39—Courtesy LC; Culver. 40, 41—Courtesy LC. 42, 43—Top: courtesy LC; center: Culver; bottom: courtesy LC except left. 44, 45—Courtesy LC except top center Culver.

CHAPTER 3: 46—Copied by Henry B. Beville. 48, 49—Culver; Franklin D. Roosevelt Library, Hyde Park, New York. 50, 51—Courtesy LC except bottom left Culver. 52, 53—Wide World Photos; painting by John McCrady. 54, 55—Courtesy LC; Bettmann—Culver. 56, 57—Ernest Hamlin Baker. 58, 59—Leo Choplin from Graphic House; courtesy Metro-Goldwyn-Mayer Inc. 60—Culver (2); Penguin Photo—RKO Radio Pictures Inc.; Warner Bros.—Culver—Universal; Culver; Paramount Pictures. 61—Culver—from "Snow White and the Seven Dwarfs," © Walt Disney Productions. 62, 63—Left: Culver—John Phillips; Rotofotos; right: Culver. 64, 65—Otto F. Hess.

CHAPTER 4: 66—Copied by Henry B. Beville. 68, 69—Brown; Culver—Brown; Fitzpatrick, St. Louis *Post-Dispatch*. 70, 71—From *Ding's Half Century* by J. N. Darling © 1962 by Meredith Publishing Co. Reprinted by permission of Duell, Sloan & Pearce, Affiliate of Meredith Press; Brown. 72, 73—Wide World Photos; UPI. 74, 75—Culver. 76, 77—Culver except top left Brown. 78, 79—Wide World Photos; Franklin D. Roosevelt Library, Hyde Park, New York, courtesy The Condé Nast Publications Inc. 80—Franklin D. Roosevelt Library, Hyde Park, New York—George Skadding. 81—UPI. 82—UPI except bottom Wide World Photos. 83—Thomas McAvoy. 84, 85—Thomas McAvoy—UPI; European Pictures Service; George Skadding. 86, 87—U.S. Army photo from Wide World Photos except left and top center UPI. 88, 89—Edmund B. Gerard; UPI.

CHAPTER 5: 90—Hugo Jaeger. 92, 93—Culver; Fitzpatrick, St. Louis *Post-Dispatch*. 94, 95—Courtesy LC. 96, 97—UPI; Brown. 98, 99—TIME cover by Ernest Hamlin Baker; courtesy the Philadelphia *Inquirer*—the Augusta, Ga., *Chronicle*. 100, 101—Culver except bottom right Brown. 102, 103—From the collection of David Weisman; courtesy LC. 104, 105—UPI—from the collection of David Weisman; Walter Sanders from Black Star. 106—Left: Eliot Elisofon; right: Wide World Photos—Sy Seidman. 107—UPI, Ted Kell for New York *Herald Tribune*. 108, 109—Eliot Elisofon—Wide World Photos; UPI; from the collection of David Weisman. 110, 111—Sy Seidman; David Robbins for FORTUNE—Hansel Mieth for FORTUNE.

CHAPTER 6: 114, 115—Fitzpatrick, St. Louis *Post-Dispatch*; Packer in New York *Daily Mirror*. 116, 117—Brown except left Culver. 118—Culver. 119—TIME cover by Ernest Hamlin Baker—TIME cover by Boris Chaliapin. 120—U.S. Air Force. 121—Bottom: Warshaw Collection of Business Americana. 122—Wide World Photos. 124, 125—Brown; Culver. 126, 127—Robert Capa; painting by Ogden Pleissner, photographed by Herbert Orth, property of Civic Center Commission, City of Detroit. 128, 129—Painting by Anton Otto Fischer—painting by Anton Otto Fischer, courtesy the Historical Services Division, Department of the Army, copied by Victor Amato. 130, 131—U.S. Air Force except right painting by Peter Hurd, courtesy the Historical Services Division, Department of the Army, copied by Victor Amato. 132, 133—Left: Copied by Robert Crandall Associates—UPI; right: Carl Mydans. 134, 135—Left: U.S. Army Signal Corps; U.S. Navy—U.S. Coast Guard—U.S. Army; right: Robert Capa. 136—Painting by Albert Gold, courtesy the Historical Services Division, Department of the Army, copied by Victor Amato. 137—George Silk. 138, 139—U.S. Army Signal Corps; painting by Ogden Pleissner, copied by Robert Crandall Associates.

CHAPTER 7: 140—U.S. Army from Wide World Photos. 142, 143—TIME covers by Ernest Hamlin Baker except bottom left TIME cover by Robert S. Sloan. 146, 147—TIME cover by Boris Chaliapin; from *Crusade in Europe* by Dwight D. Eisenhower. Copyright 1948 by Doubleday & Company, Inc. Used by permission of the publisher. 148, 149—Copyright 1944 Bill Mauldin; © 1964 by Milton Caniff—© 1964, King Features Syndicate, Inc.; George Baker from his book *The Sad Sack* published by Simon & Schuster, 1944. 150—UPI. 152—TIME cover by Ernest Hamlin Baker. 154, 155—U.S. Marine Corps. 156, 157—Painting by Tom Lea—Wide World Photos; painting by Dwight C. Shepler, courtesy U.S. Navy, copied by Henry B. Beville. 158, 159—Painting by Paul Sample, courtesy The Historical Services Division, Department of the Army, copied by Victor Amato; U.S. Navy. 160, 161—George Strock except top left Navy Department photo no. 80-G-52573 in the National Archives. 162, 163—Left: U.S. Navy by Barrett Gallagher; right: U.S. Navy—U.S. Air Force. 164, 165—Wide World Photos. 166, 167—U.S. Army Air Force from UPI; U.S. Navy.

Back cover—Henkin & Kesten.

174

175

PRODUCTION STAFF FOR TIME INCORPORATED

Arthur R. Murphy Jr. (Vice President and Director of Production)
Robert E. Foy, James P. Menton, Caroline Ferri and Robert E. Fraser
Text photocomposed under the direction of Albert J. Dunn and Arthur J. Dunn

✗

Printed by The Safran Printing Company, Detroit, Michigan
Bound by Rand McNally & Company, Hammond, Indiana
Paper by The Mead Corporation, Dayton, Ohio
Cover stock by The Plastic Coating Corporation, Holyoke, Massachusetts

A NEW FEDERALISM

1933-1945

In F.D.R.'s Administration more was
spent on public works and relief than
in all previous U.S. history. The
entire nation felt the impact.